THE GOOD,
THE BAD,
AND THE FUNNY

Football isn't just a lot of hard work! There are some times when it is weird, silly, or just plain amazing. And there are some moments when you can't believe that the men on the field are really human—they seem too good to be true. This is a collection of those moments—the highlights and the football follies—that any sports fan is sure to enjoy. On top of that, you will love the great photographs straight from *Sports Illustrated*—incredible shots that make you feel as if you're right there on the field!

Books by Bill Gutman

GREAT MOMENTS IN BASEBALL
GREAT MOMENTS IN PRO FOOTBALL
PRO FOOTBALL'S RECORD BREAKERS
REFRIGERATOR PERRY
STRANGE AND AMAZING BASEBALL STORIES
STRANGE AND AMAZING FOOTBALL STORIES
STRANGE AND AMAZING WRESTLING STORIES
BASEBALL'S RECORD BREAKERS
BASEBALL'S HOT NEW STARS

Available from ARCHWAY Paperbacks

STRANGE & AMAZING
FOOTBALL STORIES

Bill Gutman

AN ARCHWAY PAPERBACK
Published by POCKET BOOKS
New York   London   Toronto   Sydney   Tokyo

Photographs courtesy of *Sports Illustrated:* Walter Iooss Jr.:
pp. 6, 38, 57; Evan Peskin: p. 11; Herb Scharfman: pp. 26, 29;
Neil Leifer: p. 35; John Iacono: pp. 74, 95; Sheedy & Long:
p. 60; Heinz Kluetmeier: pp. 88, 90, 106; Richard Mackson:
p. 84; James Drake: p. 102. Photographs on pp. 18, 42
courtesy of Pro Football Hall of Fame.

AN ARCHWAY PAPERBACK *Original*

An Archway Paperback published by
POCKET BOOKS, a division of Simon & Schuster Inc.
1230 Avenue of the Americas, New York, N.Y. 10020

ISBN: 0-671-61133-X

First Archway Paperback printing September 1986

10 9 8 7 6 5

AN ARCHWAY PAPERBACK and colophon are
registered trademarks of Simon & Schuster Inc.

SPORTS ILLUSTRATED is a registered trademark of Time Inc.

Printed in the U.S.A.

CONTENTS

STRANGE &
AMAZING
FOOTBALL STORIES

Only On the Gridiron

The sport of football is an original. Though its origins can be traced back hundreds of years, it has evolved into a uniquely American game. In fact, with the immense exposure of both college and professional football on television, football has become the media sport of the 1980s.

Football fans all around the country can see their favorite teams and favorite players many times during the fall season, and if they watch long enough, they are bound to see some strange and unexpected happenings. Sometimes they will make you laugh, other times you will just wonder how something like that can occur during an ordinary football game.

But football, like all sports, is never ordinary. These kinds of strange and unusual events have been happening since the early days and often involve some of the all-time great players in the game. As you relive some of these moments now, just remember, they can happen only on the gridiron.

Anyone who has been around football for any length of time has heard the ball referred to as the "pigskin." The origin of the term goes way back and has a very literal genesis. Several hundred years ago, when many Englishmen were coming to the new land of America, the young boys began a very rough tradition that could be called a forerunner of the game of football.

The object was to kick a ball on the ground, and while there were different sets of rules, or no rules at all, many youngsters in various towns and cities gathered to participate in the game, which consisted of a lot of pushing and shoving and general mayhem. It wasn't unusual for the boys to come out of the game bruised and bloodied, but often ready for more.

It was also no coincidence that the game was usually played during the hog slaughtering season. The reason was simple. The "ball" used for this early forerunner of football was actually a pig's bladder. As strange as this may sound today, it was a tradition back then and has filtered down through the years with the term "pigskin." So while the game of football is still relatively young, its beginnings are rooted in traditions that began when our country was just a baby.

For those who feel modern-day football is a violent game, they ought to have seen some of the forerunners.

For instance, there was a traditional game of "football" that was played at almost all the larger colleges in the country. It consisted of a contest between the freshmen and the sophomores. The contest involved a ball, usually made of rubber or leather, but that was about the closest it came to resembling modern-day football.

The game was nothing more than a brawl, with punching, kicking, clawing, and gouging. The object, somewhere in the midst of the mess, was to push the ball through one of the groups of combatants. If the ball somehow emerged at the rear of one of the packs, the game was over. It was such a rough tradition that at Harvard University the day it was played was known as "Bloody Monday."

Amazingly, this tradition continued right up to the time of the Civil War. A rudimentary form of football was just around the corner, and college authorities finally abolished their Bloody Monday mayhem. Some traditions die hard and others are born slowly. None of those playing their own game of "football" could possibly have imagined the game played today, with artists such as Joe Montana, Eric Dickerson, and Dan Marino rewriting the record books.

The early days of college football also produced some unbelievable events. For instance, on October 7, 1916, a rag-tag team of players from little Cumberland College traveled to Atlanta to face the Ramblin' Wreck from Georgia Tech University. Cumberland had a tough, small college team at the turn of the century but shortly after had decided to concentrate on baseball. When their 1916 baseball team met with unexpected success, college officials decided it was time to get their football program back on its feet. Thus the game with Georgia Tech.

Talk about biting off more than you can chew! The best way to describe what happened is to look at a single statistic. The Georgia Tech team had the ball in its possession thirty-two times. And each of those possessions resulted in a touchdown. Each one! Beginning to get the idea? Even though the third and fourth periods were shortened by a total of fifteen minutes, it was the most one-sided game in football history. Georgia Tech defeated Cumberland by a score of 222–0!

Tech didn't bother throwing the ball. They simply rushed twenty-nine times and scored on nineteen of those carries. They had 501 yards on the ground and an average gain of 17.3 yards per carry. In addition, they scored touchdowns on five of six interceptions, five of nine punt returns, two of three fumble recoveries and on one kickoff return.

By the end of the first period it was 63–0, and by halftime, 126–0. But Tech must have been tiring, for in the abbreviated third and fourth periods they scored 54 and 42 points for the 222 total. If nothing else, Cumberland found out it needed some work on its program. But perhaps the most optimistic statement of all time came from Cumberland's Charlie Warwick, who had one pass reception for four yards and returned a kick for five more on that fateful October day long ago.

"I think we were sort of getting to them in that last quarter," Warwick quipped. Now to think like that after a 222–0 pasting is really amazing.

Sometimes even the great early players would use some unusual means to try to get their opposition to *think* a game was going to be one-sided. When the great Jim Thorpe began playing for the Canton Bulldogs, there were always many people betting on the games. It was especially true when Canton was scheduled to play archrival Massillon.

Thorpe often feigned illness or injury before the Massillon games so that the rival club would have a false sense of security. Then the news of Thorpe's ailments also would affect the odds on the games, and a great deal of money would be bet with the expectation that Jim wouldn't be playing. But just before game time, there would be the great Jim Thorpe, fit as a fiddle and rarin' to go.

Thorpe was such a physical player that some opponents claimed he wore pieces of steel in his shoulder pads so that he could hand out more punishment. But it was just Jim's hitting that caused the pain. Though he excelled in every phase of the game, Jim especially loved playing defense so he could deliver his bone-crushing tackles.

One rival said being hit by Jim Thorpe was like being hit with the blunt end of a telephone pole. And another, hit by the full fury of a Thorpe tackle, looked up to see the smiling Indian looking down at him.

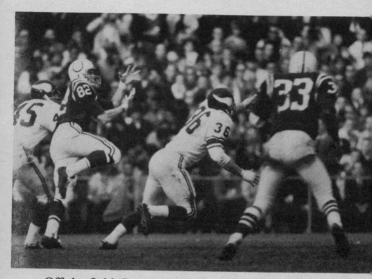

Off the field, Raymond Berry had his wife throw the passes. On game days, he was usually on the receiving end of John Unitas's passes. Here Berry (82) prepares to grab one during a 1959 game against Minnesota.

"A man could get hurt playing this game," Jim said, "if he doesn't take care."

To some players, gaining an advantage on their opponents doesn't always mean deception or trickery. Take the case of Raymond Berry, the great pass receiver for the Baltimore Colts in the late 1950s and 1960s. Berry was the favorite target of quarterback John Unitas, and the two formed one of the greatest passing combos in National Football League history.

But Raymond Berry didn't have the natural physical attributes of many of the league's top receivers. He was tall enough at 6′ 2″, but he was a thin 185 pounds and he didn't have great strength. He lacked the blazing speed of many top wideouts and wore contact lenses during games. In addition, he wore a corset to protect a fragile back.

How, then, did Raymond Berry become one of the most productive pass receivers in NFL history? The secret was dedication and practice. In fact, Raymond Berry may have practiced more than any receiver before or since. He practiced catching the ball from every conceivable angle. He practiced running his patterns until each one was precisely orchestrated to perfection. And he practiced coordinating his patterns with quarterback Unitas until the two knew each other like a pair of matched bookends.

In fact, Raymond Berry practiced so much that he often ran out of people willing to throw passes to him. For a while he fretted over the situation. Then he found an answer. The resourceful wide receiver found his own personal passer—his wife, Sally! It might have been a first.

"Sally's got a good arm," Berry would say whenever someone questioned the tactic. Anyone watching their workout agreed. Sally Berry wasn't going to put John Unitas out of a job, but she threw crisp ten- to fifteen-yard passes with good accuracy, more than enough to give her husband the kind of practice sessions he craved. She threw the ball just where he wanted it—high, low, behind him, over his head, right, left, again and again and again.

The practices were extremely important to Berry, who felt that all the good habits and good instincts had to be absorbed in practice. "In a game there's no time to think. Good practice habits keep you toned up and you do certain things without thinking in the games."

Berry's good habits made him the best split end of his day. He was instrumental in helping the Colts to NFL titles in 1958 and '59. In 1960 he had his best season with seventy-four catches for 1,298 yards and ten touchdowns. And his career stats place him among the pass receiving elite. Always a stickler for detail, Berry didn't change his habits when he became head coach of the New England Patriots midway through the 1984 season. Perennial underachievers, the Patriots of recent vintage had never seemed to live up to preseason expectations. Berry was not only instrumental in turning the team around in '84, but in 1985 he surprised the entire pro football world by leading the upstart Pats all the way to the Super Bowl. Observers claimed that Berry's careful preparation and insistence on meticulous practice habits were crucial in enabling the team to put it all together. Bidding to become only the second wild-card team in NFL history to win the Super Bowl, the Pats were short-circuited in the final game by the rough, tough Chicago Bears.

Raymond Berry's pro coaching career is still ahead of him, but no matter what the future holds, nothing will ever dim his achievements as a player. On the gridiron his so-called eccentricities contributed to his success as much as anything else. For instance, to avoid jamming his thumbs, he built up their strength by squeezing Silly Putty in his spare time. But of all the things Raymond Berry did to gain an advantage on the gridiron, perhaps the most important was proposing to a girl who had a durable and accurate throwing arm. Sally Berry might have been the most important quarterback in Raymond Berry's football life.

Like all the other sports, football has had its share of strange personalities. Flakes, they are usually called. The majority of these individuals, strange as they may be, can still function within the framework of their teams. But occasionally, one comes along who cannot.

Perhaps the most notable example of the latter was also the most aptly named. He was Joe Don Looney, and when he came out of the University of Oklahoma, he was an all-American running back, 6' 1", 224 pounds of fury who could run the hundred-yard dash in

9.8 seconds. But while Joe Don Looney could weave or power his way to touchdowns with the best of them, there were other things to consider.

Looney never graduated from Oklahoma. He got his walking papers after slugging a student assistant coach. And before becoming a Sooner, he had made stops at Texas, TCU, and a junior college in Oklahoma. Wherever Joe Don Looney went, trouble seemed sure to follow.

Yet the New York Giants had to take only one look at his gridiron statistics and considerable potential to make him their top draft choice before the 1964 season. They hoped a maturing Looney would leave his college pranks behind and become a solid citizen.

Looney forged a career with the Giants, all right, a career that lasted all of twenty-eight days. By then, the Giants realized that Looney was operating on a different wavelength from everyone else. He wouldn't listen to the coaches, didn't cooperate with the team's public relations department, refused to listen to the trainer and have his ankles taped, and missed bed checks. So after a month of preseason camp he was shipped to Baltimore.

There, he promptly took off on a brilliant, 58-yard touchdown run in an exhibition game, and once more football people began predicting big things for the big guy. But by November he was in trouble again, slugging someone and actually coming to trial. He was given probation, but by the end of the season Coach Don Shula had seen enough and Looney was off to Detroit.

As a collegian at Oklahoma, Joe Don Looney often broke away for long gains, as he does here during the 1963 season. As a pro, he went from team to team, unable to settle down, and soon found himself out of football after a series of off-field incidents.

Once again the scenario was repeated. The Lions looked at Joe Don's immense natural talent and decided to build their rushing game around him, with talk of a 1,000-yard season. A couple of great games in the preseason only strengthened the Lions' feeling that Joe Don could be their main man.

But soon there was another off-field brawl, and then a bum back, and finally clashes with the coach. The latest honeymoon for Looney ended in September of 1966, when the coach asked Joe Don to bring a play in to the quarterback.

"If you want a messenger," Joe Don supposedly said, "make a call to Western Union."

Goodbye Detroit, hello Washington. For a while, anyway. Then it was goodbye Washington, hello United States Army. After that, a quick stop at New Orleans, and the football odyssey of Joe Don Looney was over. The funny part was he didn't seem to care. He just continued to go his own way. At one point he dropped out of sight and later surfaced as a vegetarian with a personal guru studying religion. From a rock-hard 224 pounds of pure muscle, Joe Don had melted down to 180 pounds. But he seemed healthy and happy, and that's all that really matters.

As a football player, Joe Don Looney had as much potential as any running back who ever came down the pike. It's too bad NFL fans never got to really see him do his thing. But like so many other super flakes, Joe Don frittered it away, and he did it in one of the strangest ways ever seen.

* * *

There have certainly been some mighty strange players on the gridiron, but there have been strange games as well. And perhaps the strangest was the NFL title game way back in 1932. That was the last year of a single division. The following year there were Eastern and Western conferences, and the birth of the modern National Football League. But the last title game in a single division made history.

In fact, there was only a title game that year because the Chicago Bears and Portsmouth Spartans finished the regular season with 6-1-6 and 6-1-2 records, respectively. But ties were thrown out then, so each team had a 6-1 record and had to play once more for the title. The game was scheduled for Wrigley Field in Chicago. But several days before the game was to be played, the Windy City was hit by a blizzard and a cold wave. The frigid field was deemed unplayable.

That's when league officials made a strange and amazing decision. They decided to move the game to Chicago Stadium. What was so strange? Chicago Stadium was an indoor arena, usually the site of ice hockey games and various special events. The floor of the arena was not nearly the size of a football field.

But sure enough, the two clubs came indoors to play, and 11,198 fans crowded in to witness the event. Strangely enough, had the game been played outdoors, perhaps only half that many people would have attended. But it was a novelty, and for good reason.

The field was barely eighty yards long as compared to the one hundred yards of a regulation gridiron. The end zones were rounded at the corners to conform to the boards of the indoor arena. And the goalposts were moved from the end line to the goal line. When a play ended near the sideline, the ball was brought close to midfield to prevent the players from crashing into the walls that stood along the sidelines.

Fortunately, there was dirt on the floor of the arena because the circus had been performing there. It would have been even tougher if the players had played on a concrete floor. The game turned into a hard-fought contest, since neither team had much maneuverability on the small field, and the two teams battled to a scoreless tie for the first three periods.

Then in the fourth period the Bears got a break. Dick Nesbitt intercepted a pass by the Spartans' Ace Gutowsky and returned it all the way to the Portsmouth seven-yard line. On first down, the immortal Bronko Nagurski cracked for six yards to the one. Then on the next two plays, the Spartans did the impossible. They held the pile-driving Nagurski for no gain. It was fourth and goal from the 1.

Working out of the old single-wing formation, Nagurski took the direct snap about five or six yards behind the center. He started forward as if he was going to run up the middle again. Suddenly, he pulled up, took a couple of steps back, and tossed a quick pass to another gridiron immortal, Red Grange. The man known as the Galloping Ghost cradled the ball in the

14

end zone for a score. The kick made it 7–0, and a safety minutes later made it 9–0. That's the way it ended.

It was a strange game, all right, but surprisingly it resulted in some rule changes. Even in outdoor games the following year the ball was brought in from the sidelines toward the middle of the field after a play was stopped. And the goalposts were moved from the end line of the end zone to the goal line, as they had been that day at Chicago Stadium. It wasn't until thirty years or so later that they were again moved to the end line.

Today, indoor games are as common as holding penalties. Every fan knows about all the great indoor stadiums around the country—the Astrodome, the Superdome, the Silverdome, the Kingdome, and the Metrodome. But it started way back in 1932. That was the first indoor game, a strange contest that could happen only on the gridiron.

Some Kind of Tough

Tough! That simple word perhaps above all others symbolizes the game of football. It's what gives the sport its charisma, its identity, and it's a quality all the great ones have. No matter how talented, how elusive, how highly skilled a player, there comes a time when he's got to show that one special quality—tough. If he doesn't, the word soon gets out and that player will have lost his edge.

Some stories of gridiron toughness are legendary, others little known. Both bear retelling, for it's sometimes hard to believe that mortal men can be so rugged, rise to the occasion, and exhibit a kind of toughness that can only be found in football.

Perhaps football's first family of tough were the Nessers from Columbus, Ohio. They were an immi-

In the early days, the first family of pro football, had to be the Nessers. For a number of years, all six Nesser brothers played ball at the same time. Here, they are wearing the uniform of the Columbus (Ohio) Panhandles circa 1915. Left to right they are Ted, John, Phil, Al, Frank, and Fred.

grant family that came to this country before the turn of the century. Setting up house in Columbus, the Nessers became boilermakers, working for the Pennsylvania Railroad. And before long they found themselves attracted to the rugged game of football, still in its infancy.

None of the Nessers went to college, but by the second decade of the century, professional teams were springing up here and there, and the Ohio area was one of the hot spots. By 1911, the Columbus Panhandles had six Nessers in the starting lineup: Ted, John, Phil, Frank, Al, and Fred. Their father served as a combination of trainer and waterboy, while their mother did a lot of cooking and cleaning for the team.

In addition, because the Nessers worked for the railroad, the team could travel without train fare, and this helped keep the club going while other teams failed financially. One thing the Nessers had in common on the gridiron was toughness. A look at early photos shows the same steel-jawed, determined look on all of their faces.

The Nessers played for many teams before they quit. They all loved the game and knew how to play. Phil Nesser has been described as a fine all-around athlete who, under different circumstances, would have had scholarship offers from many colleges. John Nesser was a top quarterback in his day, while Frank could punt the football from one end of the field to the other, à la Jim Thorpe.

But the toughest of the Nessers had to be Al. He could throw a forward pass but was better known as a fearless defensive player who would take on Goliath himself if it meant helping his team. And despite the kind of all-out game he played, Al Nesser had a simple dictum when it came to his sport.

"Football," he said, "was made for everyone to enjoy."

Al Nesser enjoyed it, all right. He played from the

time he was a boy, turned professional in 1910, and stayed in the game until 1931, when he still played a tough end position for the old Cleveland Indians.

And when you want to talk about tough, Al Nesser wrote the book. In all the years he played football, he reportedly never wore any pads—not even a helmet. Yet he was always at the center of the action on offense and defense, taking on men much bigger than he was. So when it came to tough, Al Nesser was the equal of anyone who ever played the game.

All the great running backs in football history have been tough. There's no other way they could take such a tremendous physical pounding each game and still come back for more. And each time they carry the football there's a possibility of getting the kind of injury that could end a career. Steve Van Buren, the first of the great modern running backs, was no exception.

After an outstanding career at Louisiana State University, the 6' 1", 200-pound Van Buren joined the Philadelphia Eagles of the NFL in 1944. Though he had 9.8 speed in the hundred, the Flying Dutchman, as he was called, was also a runner of tremendous power. As a rookie, he gained 444 yards on 80 carries in just four full games and parts of two others. A year later he rambled for 832 yards on 143 carries for a 5.8 average per run. He also scored eighteen touchdowns and did all this while playing full time on defense.

In 1947, Van Buren broke the existing NFL rushing

record by gaining 1,008 yards on 217 carries. And two years later he set another mark with 1,146 yards on 263 carries. That was a monumental achievement, a tribute to Van Buren's toughness. Even today, 263 carries by a runner takes strength and endurance. But today's runners play just one way. Van Buren did it while playing the full sixty minutes without rest. And he didn't loaf for a minute on defense, either.

"Van was one of the best defensive players I ever saw," said his longtime coach Earl "Greasy" Neale. "He would constantly run through two or three blockers to make a tackle."

It was the Dutchman's toughness and determination that made it all possible. His determination can be seen by one great play he made in 1946. Coming into a game with the Detroit Lions, Van Buren was sick with a fever and bad cold. But he wouldn't sit out, preferring to play in spots as long as he could go.

With the ball at the Eagle 35, Van Buren took a handoff and started upfield. Suddenly, the crowd was on its feet. Van Buren was making one of the great broken field runs of all time. He was zigzagging back and forth across the field, eluding defenders by both finesse and power. Five times he was knocked off his feet, only to get up and run some more. In those days, ball carriers had to be pinned before the whistle blew.

Finally, the Dutchman crossed the goal line. It went into the books as a 65-yard TD run, but as Lion coach Gus Dorais said:

"It was the greatest run I ever saw. Van Buren was

sick that day, but he wouldn't be stopped. By the time he crossed the goal line he must have run more than two hundred yards back and forth across the field."

Then there was Van Buren's toughness. The Eagles quarterback in those days was Allie Sherman, later the coach of the New York Giants. In a game against Pittsburgh, one of the Steeler defenders was playing an obviously dirty brand of football and sticking it to the Eagle players all afternoon. Finally, late in the game, Steve Van Buren decided to take things into his own hands. When the Eagles came into the huddle, he asked Sherman to run the 39 play, which would give him the ball and run him right at the Pittsburgh defender who was playing it dirty.

"After I agreed to the play," Sherman recalled, "Van surprised all of us. He told both his blockers to lay off, not to block this guy at all. 'Let him through,' he told us. 'He's my private pigeon.' We all knew how serious Van was, so I gave him the go-ahead."

Van Buren took the handoff and went straight at his man. There was a tremendous collision, and when it cleared Van Buren was still running, some twenty yards downfield.

"Steve had hit the guy, just stomped all over him," Sherman said. "I'll never forget the sight. The guy was on the ground, out, and his eyes were actually spinning like pinwheels."

Though a knee injury forced him into retirement in 1952 at the early age of thirty-one, Van Buren left behind a wealth of rushing records. Maybe most of them have been broken today, but those who saw him will never forget Steve Van Buren. The Flying Dutchman was one tough football player.

Whenever football people talk about tough backs, an oldtimer will mention the name of Bronko Nagurski. The first thing that comes to mind is that the guy must have been tough to get a nickname like Bronko. Bronko Nagurski might have been the toughest man ever to play the game.

For one thing, the 235-pounder could have played any position on the field. He was usually a fullback on offense and linebacker on defense and was often described as the most destructive blocker and runner of his time.

It was also said that no one man ever tackled Nagurski, unless the tackler managed to cut Bronko's feet out from under him. He ran with his head down and his trunk nearly horizontal with the ground. He pumped his knees high, almost to his chest, so there was very little for tacklers to grab at as he plowed through the line.

Nagurski was capable of blocking two, three, and sometimes more men on a single play, and often started games at tackle before shifting to fullback. Some still say that no one ever hit harder than the Bronko, and this was never more in evidence than in a 1933 game when Bronko's Chicago Bears were playing the Philadelphia Eagles.

Bronko was carrying the ball when a rugged Philly

linebacker named John "Bull" Lipski zeroed in for the tackle. BAM! There was one of those bone-shattering collisions that can only occur on a football field. When it cleared, Nagurski was still running, but Lipski was out cold. They helped the Bull off the field, but minutes later he was back to try again.

Sure enough, Bronko carried again and Lipski tried to stop him. The result was a videotape replay long before there were videotape replays. Nagurski was still running, and Lipski was out cold . . . again. Two Philly substitutes came out to take Lipski off the field.

As they neared the sidelines, the next play began. The Bears were running a sweep, and this time Nagurski was out front leading the blocking. At the sideline, the two Philly players were still trying to get Lipski off the field. But the Bull had partially regained his senses and wanted to get back in the game.

Suddenly, all three were hit by a Mack truck that was Bronko Nagurski. All three were sent flying into the Philly bench, and poor Bull Lipski was knocked out for a third time.

Bears owner-coach, the late George Halas, never forgot that day and always chuckled about it for years afterward.

"Bronko knocked the same guy out three times in one game," he said. "That's got to be a record that will stand until another Nagurski comes along, if one ever does."

Well, one hasn't. There have been many tough football players since that time, but no one has ever quite been like Bronko Nagurski. He was as tough as they come.

Two-way football was the norm back in Bronko Nagurski's day. You didn't play the game unless you were willing to put yourself into the grinder on both offense and defense. But by the late 1940s, the two-way player began to disappear. Those who remained were tough, hard men, willing to endure the pounding for the full sixty minutes. Chuck Bednarik, the last of the two-way players in the NFL, was such a man.

He joined the Philadelphia Eagles in 1949 after an outstanding career at the University of Pennsylvania. There, he earned both All-America honors and the Maxwell Trophy as the country's outstanding college football player.

The 6' 3", 235-pound Bednarik came into the NFL at a time when two-way players were being phased out. Veterans such as Bulldog Turner were still doing a sixty-minute turn, but the young players were concentrating on either offense or defense and developing their skills to a higher level. With players specializing in just one thing, they would learn to do it better. Plus, they had a chance to rest when their unit was off the field.

So Chuck Bednarik joined the Eagles as a center. He did a fine job as a rookie, but the coaches saw he also had outstanding linebacking skills. That's where their biggest need was and in 1950, his second year, Chuck Bednarik switched to defense as a linebacker. He

Hall of Famer Chuck Bednarik (60) played both center and linebacker in the Eagles 1960 championship victory over Green Bay.

quickly became a tough, all-pro performer at that position, gaining all-league honors seven times before 1958.

That year another need arose, and the Eagles switched their versatile veteran back to center. Then came 1960, and the Eagles had a fine, contending team led by veteran Norm Van Brocklin at quarterback and the 35-year-old Bednarik, playing in his final season. Once again Chuck was the regular center. Then came the fifth game of the season against the Cleveland Browns, with Bednarik ready to anchor the offensive line as usual at center.

The Browns took the opening kickoff, and on the first play from scrimmage, Philly lost linebacker Bob Pellegrini to a groin pull. His back-up was also injured, and Coach Buck Shaw quickly scanned the bench. His eyes quickly settled on old number 60.

"Get in there at linebacker, Chuck," he said. "But don't be a hero. We need you in one piece."

So the old man trotted onto the field on defense. There were no more two-way players in the NFL, but suddenly, one of its oldest was being asked to double up. It didn't take long for the Browns to go after Bednarik. They figured the combination of his age and the fact that he hadn't played much linebacker for a couple of years would work against him. Plus, if they got him out of the game, the Eagles would be lacking a center, too.

Early in the second period he was flattened by a blind-side block that nearly put him in never-never land. As he staggered to his feet he saw Cleveland coach Paul Brown clapping his hands.

"It seemed as if they were making fun of me," Bednarik recalled, "an old man trying to play two positions. Right then and there I started playing twice as hard."

The Eagles rallied to win the game, 31–29, and when it was crunch time late in the season, with the division title on the line, Bednarik went both ways in two more games. That caused even Paul Brown to reconsider his initial assessment of the old man.

"Chuck is a great two-way player," the veteran coach said. "He is truly amazing."

But there was one more game to be played. The Eagles had taken the Eastern Conference title and were in the NFL championship game against the Green Bay Packers, a team that had surprised everyone by winning the Western Division under head coach Vince Lombardi. And before that final game, Coach Shaw once again asked Chuck Bednarik to go both ways.

It was a heavy burden to place on a 35-year-old, especially in a title game, with the play more intense and the hitting harder. Bednarik was more than willing to do it. After all, just one more game and he could go home and rest. Only he wanted to rest as a champion.

Some 67,000 fans at Franklin Field in Philadelphia knew what was happening after the first series of downs, in which the Packers intercepted a Van Brocklin pass. Eleven members of the Green Bay de-

The hard-nosed Bednarik is generally considered the last of the two-way players. Whether on offense or defense, number 60 was always in the thick of the action, always an impact player.

fense trotted off the field, and ten members of the Eagles offense left. Only number 60 remained, a stoic figure standing alone on the gridiron. The fans roared. They knew immediately that Chuck Bednarik was waiting for the rest of the Eagles. Once again he was going both ways.

It was a rugged, physical game all the way. Green Bay took an early 6–0 lead on a pair of Paul Hornung field goals. But Philly bounced back. A pair of Van Brocklin to Tommy McDonald passes produced a touchdown, and a Bobby Walston field goal made it 10–6 in favor of the Eagles by half time. Chuck had been in for every play, and his pass blocking on the Van Brocklin to McDonald passes had been outstanding.

In the third period he stopped a Packer drive with a vicious tackle of Paul Hornung that put the Golden Boy on the sidelines for part of the period. But at the outset of the final period the Pack scored again on a Bart Starr to Max McGee pass that gave Lombardi's troops a 13–10 lead.

Then midway through the final session the Eagles drove for another score and a 17–13 advantage. Green Bay tried to come back. They started one drive, but Max McGee fumbled after catching a Starr pass, and there was a pileup near midfield. When they unstacked, Chuck Bednarik was clutching the football at the Philly 48. He had saved the day once again.

In the final minutes, Bednarik's body ached from the pounding he had taken by going both ways. But he dug in as the Packers began driving again. With fifteen seconds left, the Pack was on the Eagle 22. Quarterback Starr dumped a pass off to his powerful fullback, Jim Taylor. Taylor eluded one tackler and powered past another. He had crossed the 10-yard line with the goal and winning score just a few steps away.

But at the nine there was a collision. The screaming Philly fans saw Taylor caught in a bear hug by number 60. Chuck Bednarik wrestled Taylor to the ground and held him there as time ran out. The Eagles were champions!

During the postgame hoopla, Eagles coach Buck Shaw put things in perspective. He told the press flat out that the Eagles wouldn't have won the game without Chuck Bednarik.

"We've got to thank the old man," he said. "He held us together on offense and defense. It was simply an amazing performance by an amazing athlete."

That it was. For Chuck Bednarik, the last of the two-way players, was one tough guy.

It takes only a few stories from the gridiron to convince people that football players are a breed apart, with a special kind of toughness that ordinary people don't possess. Players play the game with the kind of pain that would put office workers on the shelf. And it was worse in the old days, when sports medicine wasn't even in its infancy.

Knee operations, for example, were very rare in football's early years. If a player hurt a knee he just continued to play until it was impossible. There was often the risk of permanent damage, but the old-time player didn't really consider that when it was time to suit up.

Steve Van Buren was one superstar whose career was ended by a knee injury. When the great Eagles halfback was hurt, his knee was put in a cast—no operation. Van Buren then left the cast on too long and the knee calcified. In working overtime to break the adhesions, Van Buren developed a spur on the inside of his toe. In addition, he had lost mobility. Had Van Buren played today, the injury might have been relatively minor because of more advanced medical procedures.

But as Sammy Baugh, the great Redskins quarterback, said, "We were all leery of knee operations back when I played. If we got hurt, we'd just crip around and try to play anyway."

Hall of Fame fullback Ernie Nevers remembers his Chicago Cardinal team going out with just sixteen men one year. The players just couldn't afford to get hurt.

"There was one guy with a trick knee," Nevers recalled. "Before the games he'd always remind us that if he went down and couldn't get back up, that someone had to jerk his knee back in place so he could keep playing."

That's toughness. Toughness was also Tommy Thompson of Tulsa, the Eagles quarterback in the 1940s, who practiced his passing hours and hours on end to compensate for his lack of depth perception.

You see, Tommy Thompson was virtually blind in one eye, yet he got so he could throw long passes with pinpoint accuracy.

Toughness was middle linebacker Ray Nitschke of Green Bay playing his heart out against the Giants in the 1962 NFL title game and leading the Packers to a 16–7 victory on an ice-swept Yankee Stadium tundra. Nitschke was the game's Most Valuable Player for his efforts, but when he showed people his hands that night, they couldn't believe the sight.

The freezing cold had made the skin raw and bleeding. His hands were also so swollen that flesh completely covered a ring he was wearing. That's pain, but Nitschke never complained.

Tough was Jim Brown, the man considered the greatest running back ever. It wasn't all those rushing records that made him so tough. It was the fact that in nine seasons, carrying the ball nearly 2,400 times and gaining more than 12,000 yards, Jimmy Brown never missed a ball game. He was so strong that he often had to be gang tackled, buried under six or eight hundred pounds of defense. Yet he was never seriously hurt and always ready to play. .

Tough was Red Cagle, an all-American at Army who never had quite the same success in pro ball when he played in the 1930s. But Cagle had flair. He rarely wore a helmet, and his flaming red hair made him an easy man to spot and a fan favorite. On those occasions when he paid the price for not having the protective headgear, Cagle would simply wrap a bandage around his head to keep the blood out of his eyes and return to action—still without a helmet!

So there have been all kinds of tough in football. The tradition continues today.

Sometimes football toughness is carried off the gridiron. Several NFL stars have come back from injuries suffered away from football to play again. But it takes a kind of determination that NFL players have made famous.

Jerry Kramer was one of the National Football League's premier guards in the 1960s. Playing for the Green Bay Packer juggernaut, Kramer teamed with fellow guard Fuzzy Thurston to lead Paul Hornung and Jim Taylor around the ends on a sweep play that perhaps was the most effective ever run. It was also Kramer who made the famous block with 13 seconds left against Dallas enabling Packer quarterback Bart Starr to score the winning touchdown in the 1967 NFL title game.

Yet it was a tribute to Kramer's toughness that he was playing football at all. When he was seventeen years old he was chasing a runaway calf across his family's property, and he stepped on the end of an old rotting plank. Somehow, the wood sprung upward and slivers entered Kramer's body where his leg joined his torso.

The youngster pulled a long sliver out himself, then went home. But when the pain started, he went to a doctor. At first, X rays showed nothing, but finally

Green Bay quarterback Bart Starr (15) hands the ball to halfback Travis Williams (23) during the Packers NFC title game against Dallas in 1967. It was Starr who later scored the winning touchdown in the final seconds behind a Jerry Kramer block.

another exam showed a foreign object. This time a seven-inch-long sliver was removed. It had just missed a major artery and his spine by a whisker. But being young and strong, Kramer recovered and went on to a successful high school, college, and then pro career.

He was already an all-pro guard at the end of the 1963 season, a big part of the Packer title teams and in his prime. But before 1964 began, Kramer began to have severe abdominal pain once again. After somehow playing the first game of the season, Kramer had to submit to surgery. Incredibly, that was the first of eight operations that left Jerry Kramer fighting for his life, let alone a football career.

The culprit was that same accident that had occurred twelve years earlier. There were still undetected slivers of wood in his body, and they had shifted enough to begin causing major problems. It took all those operations to finally make him well.

No one thought Jerry Kramer would play football again, let alone be able to take the pounding in the trenches. But by 1965 he was back building up his strength. There were so many surgical scars on his abdomen that his teammates took to calling him "the Zipper." But by the end of the season he was playing his usual major role in the Packers' drive to another NFL title. It was an amazing recovery, an incredible testimony to his toughness. No wonder Jerry Kramer ended up in pro football's Hall of Fame.

* * *

Then there was Billy Kilmer. Most fans remember him as the gutty quarterback of the Washington Redskins in the 1970s, a player without flashy natural skills, but with a heart as big as a mountain. Kilmer wore his emotions on his sleeve and inspired an aging offense to perform beyond its years. Statistically, he didn't rank with some of the great ones, but he was a leader whose teammates would follow him anywhere. You can't ask much more than that from a quarterback.

But Kilmer had still another quality. He was tough, and in his case it can be spelled with a capital *T*. Though Billy Kilmer exhibited his toughness many times on the gridiron, he actually would not have been playing at all if he hadn't shown even more toughness and determination to overcome adversity off the gridiron.

It happened at the end of the 1962 season, Billy's second with the San Francisco 49ers. He had come out of UCLA as an all-American tailback, and since the 49ers were putting in a new formation, the shotgun, they wanted a quarterback who could run as well as pass and was used to taking a long snap from center. With the Niners, Kilmer split duties with two other QBs, veteran John Brodie and young Bobby Waters. Brodie was the pure passer, Waters more the runner, and Kilmer a combination of both. Billy did just moderately well, as did the shotgun.

Only Billy never finished that 1962 season. With two games remaining, he left a practice session to drive back to the city. He never made it. He either fell asleep

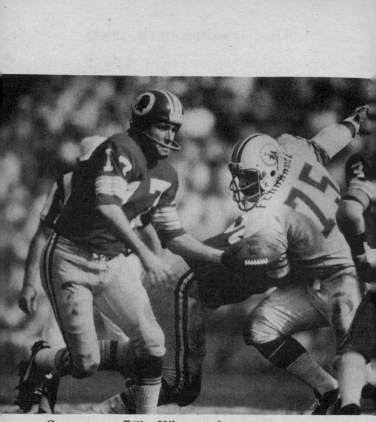

Courageous Billy Kilmer, who overcame a severe leg injury to become a star quarterback for the Washington Redskins, shown in action against Miami in Super Bowl VII. Though he didn't have the physical ability of others, Kilmer was a great leader who often found a way to get the job done.

at the wheel or another car cut in front of him. Billy couldn't remember, because suddenly his car was careening down a steep embankment, rolling some 435 feet through a field and into a deep ditch.

Kilmer's right leg was badly fractured, and he was suffering from other injuries as well. By the time rescue workers arrived to get him out, muddy water from the ditch had started an infection in the broken leg. He was not in good shape.

At first, the doctors weren't sure they could save the leg. Once that crisis passed, Billy asked about walking. They told him he would probably never walk normally again. Then he asked them about playing football. No way, the doctors said. There was no chance he could ever play again.

Billy Kilmer took a deep breath. On this count, he knew the doctors were wrong. He'd play again, no matter what it took to get there. For starters, it took three months in the hospital. Then shortly after he hobbled home, Billy had to return for another operation, this one to remove some floating bone chips. The rest of the rehabilitation was up to him.

He didn't play at all in 1963, didn't even attempt it. But in the back of his mind every waking minute were thoughts of a comeback. He knew he'd have to tough it out.

"My whole life to then had been athletics," he said. "I figured I was just too young to give it all up. And when I make up my mind about something, I tend to get a little stubborn about it."

So Billy Kilmer worked. He put in hours of sweat and pain as his ankle and leg came around slowly. But it came. And to the surprise of everyone, Billy Kilmer reported to the 49ers camp prior to the 1964 season. That, in itself, was amazing.

Though he came back to play without pain, Billy found himself without a position. The Niners were no longer using the shotgun, and the team decided to try him at running back. In the first scrimmage he was the leading runner with thirty-seven yards on seven carries. It was an incredible achievement, considering the condition of his leg just two years earlier.

Kilmer didn't make his mark as a quarterback until he was traded to the expansionist New Orleans Saints in 1967, and he didn't earn all the accolades until his Redskin career began in 1971. But he wound up playing until he was nearly forty, and playing on a leg that had been so badly broken years earlier that they said he'd never play again. But the toughness of Billy Kilmer was never to be denied.

It Takes Teamwork

Teamwork. That's the magic ingredient that can spell success or failure for any venture, on or off the gridiron. But there is no denying that in football teamwork is often the final piece to the puzzle. It is the key that makes the superstars, ordinary players, and substitutes blend into a well-oiled machine.

There have been many examples of teamwork down through the years and many ways in which it has manifested itself. Of course, teamwork does not always result in victory. There is a kind of negative teamwork, whether intentional or not, that can show up in other ways. In today's game, for instance, the teamwork between player and agent can sometimes result in holdouts and walkouts, which can hurt the player and his team.

So teamwork is an interesting phenomenon, one

The legendary Jim Thorpe will always be among the greatest who ever played.

which bears some scrutiny to see how it has affected the gridiron game in the course of its history.

Though all players know the value of teamwork, some, more than others, have a difficult time accepting that fact on a full-time basis. For various reasons a player can become a "maverick" and decide to do things his own way. The great Jim Thorpe was sometimes one of these mavericks. No one could ever predict when the great Indian athlete would tire of one situation and decide to move on.

In the early 1920s, when the National Football League was still trying to get a foothold with the fans, franchises came and went with the setting of the sun. Jim Thorpe was playing and starring for the powerful Canton Bulldogs, but he was getting restless. He began missing games and sometimes just refused to play for various reasons. Finally, he decided to walk away from Canton entirely to put together a team of Indian players that would be the equal of any in the land.

It was an ambitious undertaking and perhaps the only time in football history that a team was formed strictly along racial or ethnic lines. But it didn't quite work out that way. Though Thorpe had two other outstanding Indian gridders on the club, halfback Joe Guyon and end Pete Calas, he found there really weren't enough Indian ballplayers around to make a team.

The team was already named the Oorang Indians, though, surprisingly, the name was taken from a local dog kennel. The Indians entered the league representing Marion, Ohio, with Jim acting as the coach as well as the star. But there was still the problem of getting ballplayers.

What Jim Thorpe was forced to do was find some "honorary" Indians to fill the roster, which was only eighteen players in those days. So the Oorang Indians really weren't all Indians despite the good intentions. They did, however, use names such as Running Deer, Gray Horse, Eagle Feather, Tomahawk, Little Twig, and other Indian-sounding handles. On the field they sometimes appeared in sets of feathers and with Indian costumes over their uniforms.

As a football team, however, the Oorang Indians left a little something to be desired. With the great Jim Thorpe in the lineup, they were an average team at best. Without him, they were probably not even equal to a good college team. A perfect example was the day the Oorang Indians met Akron without Jim. When the smoke cleared, Akron had completed a 66–0 romp.

Needless to say, the Oorang Indians did not remain part of the National Football League for very long.

There was still another strange team formed back in 1930, this one to answer a challenge that was made in response to some bragging by one of the greatest college football coaches of all time. He was Knute Rockne, the legendary coach who put Notre Dame football on the map to stay.

For years, Rockne had been telling anyone who would listen that he had Notre Dame clubs that could have beaten any professional football team. In those days, college and pro football were bitter rivals, as the young professional league competed for the fans with the more traditional college game.

Anyway, Rockne kept making his boast until someone finally called his bluff. In the fall of 1930, as the Great Depression was just beginning, the Rock agreed to a game pitting a team of Notre Dame all-stars against the professional New York Giants, with all the gate receipts going to help the unemployed.

Rockne decided that the Giants were big, but slow, and figured if his Irish all-stars could score two or three early touchdowns, they would have no trouble holding the Giants the rest of the way. Rockne really did assemble an all-star aggregation, but many of them were famous names from the past, such as the fabled Four Horsemen backfield. The problem was that many of these men hadn't played in years and really weren't in the kind of condition to cope with a team of physically fit professionals.

The Giants were led by Benny Friedman, an outstanding quarterback who kept a low profile before the game but who was angered by Rockne's boasts and determined to lead his team to a victory.

While the game attracted a great deal of attention, the hype was greater than the moment. It didn't take long to see that Rockne's all-stars were out of shape and overmatched. There was no way they would get that two- or three-touchdown lead Rockne had hoped for. The Giants were just too tough.

At one point, the Giants kept pushing the Four Horsemen and their mates further and further back until they had a third down and 32 to go for a first down. Even with the Notre Dame star of a year earlier, Frank Carideo, running the show, Rockne's charges could do nothing on offense.

The game was probably typified by a Benny Friedman run near the end of the second period. Though not a bruising, pile-driving runner, Benny ran right over several N.D. defenders, including Carideo, en route to a 25-yard score. There were Notre Dame players sprawled all over the field after that one.

Eyewitnesses said the Giants really could have run it up if they wanted, but once they saw how easy it was they slacked off a bit. The final was 22–0, but the tip-off was that the Notre Dame all-stars had minus 30 yards in total offense. They couldn't move the ball a lick. The game also proved once and for all that the pros were for real. They were not about to go away.

As for Knute Rockne, the game did little to take away his greatness, though he continued to say that his Notre Dame teams could beat the pros. But the game showed that sometimes all the team spirit and teamwork in the world can't make up for speed, size, condition, and execution . . . as well as teamwork.

It's an old axiom in the National Football League that on any given Sunday any team is capable of beating any other team. In other words, if conditions are right and everything clicks, the worst team in the league is capable of beating the best team. Granted, it doesn't happen too often.

But when the two best teams meet for the league title, anything can happen. Sometimes the games are hard fought and undecided until the final seconds. Other times one team dominates, and sometimes it's difficult to explain why. It's usually a combination of the game plan, execution, and teamwork. But that's always been one of the great mysteries of sport. Why does one team suddenly dominate a team that is equal in talent and ability?

Perhaps the most amazing example occurred in the 1940 championship game. It's legendary now and as utterly incredible nearly fifty years after it happened. During the regular season that year both the Chicago Bears and Washington Redskins were en route to the Western and Eastern Division titles. When they met in a midseason game, the Redskins prevailed after a hard-fought contest, 7–3. So when the two got ready to meet for the league title on December 8, at old Griffith Stadium in Washington, the Skins felt that midseason game gave them an advantage.

They also had the great Sammy Baugh at quarterback. A tall, thin Texan, Slingin' Sam was the premier passer of his day. He was as tough as nails and had a rifle arm. The Bears, however, had their own fine quarterback, Sid Luckman, and he ran the complex T-formation put in by Bears owner-coach George Halas.

The T would become standard for all teams a few years down the road, but in 1940 it was new and still under tight scrutiny.

Earlier in the season, however, Redskins' owner George Preston Marshall had given the Bears added ammunition. Said Marshall:

"The Bears are crybabies. When the going gets tough, the Bears quit."

It's never smart to give an opponent added incentive. Sometimes a remark like that can spark new-found pride and be more motivating than the money or the title. Then, a day before the game, something else happened. Some of the Redskins players hung around the field to watch the Bears practice. Running back Andy Farkas remembered what happened next.

"The Bears came out screaming like a pack of wild men," he said. "They took off and ran the length of the field. Then they circled the goalposts and ran all the way back. And they were still screaming. I'd never seen anything like it."

That was the extent of the practice. Coach Halas knew his team was psyched and ready, and he didn't want them to leave any of that madness on the practice field.

Even quarterback Luckman, relatively new to the pro game, could sense his team's feeling.

"I've never experienced anything like it," he recalled. "There was a feeling of tension in the air, as though something tremendous was about to happen."

It didn't take long. The Bears took the opening

kickoff back to the 24. After George McAfee ran for 8 yards to the 32, Luckman handed the ball to Bill Osmanski on a counter play. The big halfback raced around left end for 68 yards and a score. The kick made it 7–0.

Washington tried to bounce back. A 62-yard kickoff return by Max Krause set things up for Sammy Baugh. He immediately dropped back and fired toward Charley Malone in the end zone—but Malone dropped the ball! Then the Bears tightened up, and when they got the ball back, they promptly marched 80 yards on seventeen running plays, and Luckman scored from the one.

Twice more the Bears scored before half time, and they left the field with a 28–0 lead. Sometimes a team will ease up with a big lead, but the Bear players remembered what Marshall had said about them being a team of quitters. They came out even more determined in the second half, determined to pour it on and teach the Redskins a lesson they wouldn't forget.

The onslaught continued. The Bears ran roughshod over the Redskins all day. It seemed as if nothing could stop the Chicago steamroller. They scored twenty-six points in the third period and another nineteen in the final session. The score wound up 73–0, the most one-sided title game in NFL history.

In winning by such a monumental score, the Bears had rolled up 382 rushing yards to just 22 for the Skins. The Monsters of the Midway had shown they were indeed not a bunch of quitters. As for Sammy Baugh, who had thrown the ball fifty-one times in an attempt to generate some offense, he was asked if the outcome would have been any different if Charley Malone hadn't dropped that pass in the end zone early in the game.

"Yeah, it would have been different," Baugh said. "If he had caught the ball the score would have been 73–7."

Perhaps no team in the history of the National Football League had as much to prove as the 1950 Cleveland Browns. And because of their unique situation, the Browns exhibited a special kind of teamwork that made their final achievement a totally amazing one.

Why was 1950 such a special season for the Browns? It's simple. It was their first year in the NFL. But then again, aren't new teams in the NFL expected to struggle for a few years? Expansion teams, for instance, are usually lucky to win a single game their first year. True, but the Cleveland Browns weren't exactly a new team.

For the four previous seasons they had been part of a renegade league, the All America Football Conference. And in those four seasons the Browns dominated in a way few teams have before or since. They were the AAFC champion all four years and had an amazing 47-4-3 record during that time. In 1948, they were 14-0, and it was a rare occasion indeed when they lost a football game.

The Browns already boasted such stars as quarterback Otto Graham, fullback Marion Motley, tackle-placekicker Lou "the Toe" Groza, and receivers Mac Speedie, Dante Lavelli, and Dub Jones. The driving force behind this aggregation of stars was owner-coach Paul Brown, whom many were already calling an innovative genius.

But the AAFC folded at the end of the 1949 season, and for a short time the future of the Browns and the rest of the teams was in doubt. Then the older NFL decided to absorb three of the teams, the San Francisco 49ers, the Baltimore Colts . . . and the Cleveland Browns. The other AAFC teams, including the old New York Yankees and Brooklyn Dodgers, fell by the wayside.

Still, the NFL acted as if it were doing these three teams a favor. The older league had been treating the AAFC like a rinky-dink organization, cutting it down whenever it had the chance. While the Browns were clobbering all their AAFC opponents, someone asked a top NFL official if the two leagues would ever meet. He laughed and said the AAFC would have to get a ball first.

But now the Browns, Colts, and 49ers were in the NFL, and the pressure was mostly on the Browns. They were the team with the rep, and Paul Brown was determined not to be embarrassed. He picked up some of the top players from the defunct AAFC teams to shore up any weak points and immediately dispatched his assistants to study the NFL teams the Browns would be playing in 1950.

So on the night of September 16, 1950, the Browns were more than ready for their NFL debut. They would be playing the Philadelphia Eagles, and most NFL fans were hoping the boys from Philly would easily defend the league's honor against this upstart aggregation from the AAFC.

The Eagles scored first on a field goal, and the fans thought it was in the bag. In spite of running star Steve Van Buren's absence, it looked as if the Philly club could push the Browns around. Only the Browns were simply using the opening minutes to feel out the Eagle offense and defense and to make sure their careful scouting had gauged things correctly. Once they determined that things were just as they thought, Paul Brown's club really went to work.

On the next series, Cleveland quarterback Graham promptly hit Dub Jones on a 59-yard scoring pass. The kick made it 7–3. In the second quarter, the slick quarterback connected on a 26-yard scoring toss to Dante Lavelli, and it was a 14–3 game at half time.

In the third period, Graham engineered a beautiful drive, throwing three straight passes to a back in motion. When Philly adjusted, the QB hit Lavelli for 32 yards, then passed 12 yards to Speedie for the score. After the Eagles finally scored early in the fourth, the Browns roared back for two more, at one point scoring on eight straight running plays in a drive that covered 72 yards.

The final was 35–10, and the Browns had shown they were a force to be reckoned with in the NFL. The victory was no fluke. The Browns finished the regular season with a 10–2 mark, the same record as the New York Giants in the NFL's Eastern Division. Then they beat the Giants, 8–3, in a play-off. In their first NFL season the Cleveland Browns were in the championship game. That, in itself, was an amazing accomplishment.

In the title game they would be meeting the Los Angeles Rams, a team that had deserted Cleveland for the sun of the West Coast five years before the Browns arrived in the NFL. The Rams were a star-studded outfit, with quarterbacks Bob Waterfield and Norm Van Brocklin, receivers Tom Fears and Elroy "Crazylegs" Hirsch, and runners Glenn Davis, Verda "Vitamin" Smith, Paul "Tank" Younger, and Dan Towler. The Rams were the highest-scoring team in the league, with 466 points in twelve games. The Browns had the best defense, yielding just 144 points. Something had to give.

It did, and in a hurry. On the very first play from scrimmage, quarterback Waterfield hit halfback Davis down the left sideline, and the former Army all-American outraced the Cleveland secondary to complete an 82-yard touchdown play. And the game was just seconds old! Maybe the upstart Browns had finally met their match?

The quick strike could have demoralized a lesser team. But the Browns took it in stride, stuck to their game plan, and exploded right back. Graham drove them 72 yards in six plays to even things up, the final 32 yards coming on a pass to Dub Jones. Groza's kick made it a 7–7 game.

When the Rams got the ball, however, they showed they wouldn't roll over either. Waterfield went back to work and drove his team, hitting Fears on a 44-yard pass and then handing to Vitamin Smith, who rambled for 15. From the three, Dick Hoerner banged over and the Rams were back in front, 14–7. And they were chewing up the vaunted Browns defense.

Finally, the defenses tightened, but early in the second period the Browns scored again on a 35-yard pass from Graham to Dante Lavelli. But a bad snap from center caused the extra-point try to fail, and L.A. had a 14–13 lead. It stayed that way right until halftime.

Early in the third period the Browns took the lead for the first time when Graham hit Lavelli on a 39-yard touchdown toss, making it 20–14. But midway through the quarter the Rams struck swiftly. The first drive featured a 38-yard Waterfield to Vitamin Smith pass that took it to the 17. Then Dick Hoerner smashed into the Browns' line seven straight times and finally scored from the one. The kick made it 21–20.

After the kickoff, the Browns gave the ball to their great fullback, Marion Motley. Only this time he fumbled, and L.A.'s Larry Brink scooped it up and ran it six yards for still another score. The kick made it 28–20, and now it looked as if the Browns had run out of miracles.

It was still a 28–20 game late in the third quarter

when Cleveland's Warren Lahr intercepted a Waterfield pass. Otto Graham then engineered a long drive that resulted in a score when he passed 14 yards to Rex Bumgardner. Groza's kick made it a one-point game at 28–27.

Cleveland tried to drive again, but with about three minutes left, Graham fumbled in L.A. territory and the Rams got the ball. All they had to do was run out the clock and just one first down might do it. But the Browns' defense tightened and stopped the L.A. ground attack on three straight plays. Waterfield punted, and Cliff Lewis took the ball back to the Cleveland 32. As Graham led his offense onto the field, there was just one minute and fifty seconds left. Could the Browns do it?

They were still 68 yards from paydirt as Graham went to work. He started by running 14 yards to the 46. Then he hit Bumgardner for 15 and Dub Jones for 16 more. With a minute left, the ball was on the Los Angeles 23.

Always a cool customer under pressure, Graham promptly hit Bumgardner for 12 more yards to the Rams' 11. The QB then sneaked for a couple to get the ball in better position. With just 28 seconds left, Lou Groza kicked a 16-yard field goal to give Cleveland a dramatic 30–28 victory. The Browns had done it.

There have been other great games, other examples of teamwork in action, but none was quite as amazing as the Cleveland Browns victory in 1950. It was the first of six straight NFL title games for Paul Brown's team, and ten straight counting the four in the AAFC.

Still, that first one had to be the best. Never before or since has a team come into a new league and dominated the way the Cleveland Browns did. Not only that, they showed confidence and teamwork by coming from behind several times in the final game, a game some football people call the greatest ever played.

Miracle finishes always create quite a stir throughout the football world, and there have certainly been enough of them through the years. The old adage that says it ain't over till it's over is certainly true. Sometimes, however, the miracle finish that isn't quite a miracle attracts as much attention as the other kind.

On January 1, 1963, there was a great deal of excitement over the upcoming Rose Bowl game in Pasadena, California. It was the dream game of the season as Southern California, ranked number one in the country, went up against the University of Wisconsin, ranked second. So it was truly a game to decide the national champion and interest was at a peak.

The game began, but as the first quarter moved to the second, the second to the third, and then into the fourth, it seemed like another case of expectations far outstripping reality. The game had become a laugher and, unless you were a diehard USC fan, a colossal bore.

Led by their all-American quarterback, Pete Beathard, the Trojans were taking the Badgers apart. One minute into the final period, Beathard had thrown four

Wisconsin's Ron VanderKelen put on a great aerial show in the 1963 Rose Bowl against Southern Cal. The Badger quarterback (15) was also outstanding in the College All-Star game that year, but never became a first string signalcaller in the pros.

TD passes and USC had what seemed like an insurmountable 42–14 lead.

But then things began happening. First, Wisconsin's Lou Holland scored on a thirteen-yard run, the kick cutting the lead to 42–21. A USC fumble minutes later set the Badgers up again, and with 8:32 left, quarterback Ron VanderKelen passed four yards to Gary Kroner for another score. The kick made it 42–28. Could the impossible be happening?

Quarterback VanderKelen had been relatively quiet for three periods, but in the fourth he began looking like a combination of John Unitas and Joe Montana. He couldn't miss, and he began passing the Trojan defense silly.

It was still 42–28 with 2:40 left when a bad snap from center forced the USC punter into the end zone, where he was tackled for a safety. Now it was 42–30, and Wisconsin would be getting the ball back. Sure enough, VanderKelen passed his team right back down the field, hitting all-American Pat Richter from the 19 for yet another score. The kick made it a five-point game at 42–37. Now fans all over the country who had been bored and restless were on the edge of their collective seats.

Could Wisconsin pull off a miracle finish? The Badgers tried an onsides kick to get the ball again, but USC managed to recover. With time running out, the Trojans needed just one first down to run out the clock. But they couldn't get it and had to punt. VanderKelen and his offense came out again, but they had no timeouts remaining, and before they could run a play the gun sounded, ending the game and also one of the great comebacks of our time.

Though they had fallen five points short, Wisconsin made a run at it and quarterback VanderKelen made national headlines. He had completed eighteen of twenty-two fourth-period passes, thirty-three of forty-eight overall for 401 yards and two touchdowns. Not considered a top pro prospect before, his stock rose quickly and he was a high draft choice of the Minnesota Vikings the following season.

Unfortunately, he never attained the heights as a pro that he had in those final twelve minutes in Pasadena. After a few years as a back-up, he was out of the league. But for one quarter in a single game, VanderKelen and his teammates were as amazing as any offense had ever been before or since.

While the USC Trojans were almost victimized by an amazing Wisconsin comeback in the 1963 Rose Bowl, the 1974 Trojan squad did a little comeback number of its own, and more than a decade later, the game undoubtedly still makes Notre Dame fans wince.

Ara Parseghian's Irish squad came to California with mayhem on their minds. They were the number one defensive team in the country coming into the game, having yielded just nine touchdowns in their ten previous games. So when their offense also clicked and helped the Irish to a 24–0 lead with just minutes re-

USC halfback Anthony Davis breaks into the clear during one of his long runs in the Trojans' great comeback victory over Notre Dame.

maining in the first half, their fans relaxed. We got 'em this time, they must have thought.

Then with just seconds left in the half, USC quarterback Pat Haden hit tailback Anthony Davis with a seven-yard scoring pass, breaking the drought. The extra point try failed, so the Irish still had a 24–6 halftime lead. It wouldn't be a shutout, but with the Irish defense, the lead was still safe.

Guess again. Davis took the second half kickoff at his own goal line and stunned the Irish with a zigzagging, 100-yard return that had the huge crowd in the L.A. Coliseum cheering wildly. Another point failed, but it was now 24–12. From there, things happened rapidly.

Minutes later Davis scored again, this time from the 6, the extra point making it 24–19. A Notre Dame fumble at its own 31 enabled the Trojans to drive in again, and Davis scored from the 4. The speedy tailback then ran in a two-point conversion and it was 27–24, USC in front.

It was still the third period when a 56-yard punt return set up an 18-yard Haden to J. K. McKay pass for another score. Minutes later Haden hit McKay on a 45-yard score and both extra points upped the lead to 41–24. The Irish were in a daze, unable to comprehend just what kind of steamroller had hit them. And Southern Cal wasn't about to give them time to find out.

In the fourth period the Irish fumbled again, and Haden threw 16 yards to Sheldon Diggs for yet another score. Then Trojan defensive back Charlie Phillips picked off a Notre Dame pass and rambled 58 yards for a final tally. When it had mercifully ended, Southern Cal had taken a 55–24 victory, coming back from a 24–0 deficit to do it.

The fifty-five points had been compressed into just seventeen minutes of game action, an incredible scoring spree made even more unbelievable because it came against the top defensive team in the land. But that's the strange thing about teamwork. For one team, it all came explosively together. For the other, it never existed.

The Unexpected

It happens in every sport: plays or events that turn your head, make you sit up and take notice. Sometimes they make you laugh, a sudden turn of events with humorous overtones. But other times they can make you cry, because these unexpected happenings can cost a ball game, or even a season.

What each of these plays has in common is the element of surprise. They happen when least expected. It could be during a routine midseason game, a meaningless contest between two mediocre teams, or it could happen in a play-off or title game, when everything is on the line. It doesn't matter. The unexpected is one of the elements that makes football exciting and fun. So relax and watch the plays develop.

It was the Cotton Bowl game, January 1, 1954. The University of Alabama was facing Rice University in one of the big games of the year. The Crimson Tide was quarterbacked by Bart Starr, who would go on to become an all-time great pro with the Green Bay Packers. Rice was spearheaded by a fleet halfback, Dicky Moegle, and before the day was out, football fans would all know Moegle's name.

The Tide scored first, driving downfield with Starr giving the ball to fullback Tommy Lewis, who took it in from the one. The kick missed, but Alabama had a 6–0 lead.

Early in the second period, Moegle began to assert himself. He broke loose on a brilliant 79-yard touchdown run to tie the game. The point after made it 7–6, Rice. Then midway through the period, Alabama was driving again when Starr fumbled the ball away on the Rice 10. A backfield in motion penalty brought the ball back to the 5 and set the stage for one of the most bizarre plays in football history.

Once again the speedy Moegle got the football. After some fancy footwork at the line of scrimmage, he burst into the clear and began motoring down the right sideline. The fans roared. It was quickly obvious that Moegle was going all the way, that they were witnessing a 95-yard touchdown run in progress.

Then as Moegle raced just past midfield, it happened. A helmetless player standing in front of the Alabama bench suddenly leaped onto the playing field and tackled the speeding Moegle. Everyone stopped in a state of shock. It was 'Bama fullback Tommy Lewis, who had scored the game's first touchdown. In a pure show of football emotion, Lewis had come off the bench to make a tackle.

"I kept telling myself I didn't do it, but I knew I had," Lewis said. "I guess I was too full of Alabama."

For a few seconds everyone was speechless, including most of the huge crowd. After all, no one had ever seen a player bolt off the bench to make a stop before. Finally, the refs huddled together and made the only ruling they could. Moegle was awarded a touchdown. It would go in the books as a 95-yard scoring run.

So the game continued and Dicky Moegle continued to ramble. He broke loose for a 34-yard TD scamper in the third period and wound up with 265 yards on eleven carries, an average of 24.1 yards per jaunt. That in itself was amazing. And the final score of the game was Rice over Alabama, 28–6.

Strangely enough, the game wasn't remembered as the day Dicky Moegle ran wild or the day Rice soundly whipped Alabama. It was always remembered as the day the unexpected happened, the day an emotional young player bolted from the bench to stop a touchdown run in progress. The only problem was he didn't belong there. But who could really blame him for trying?

Tommy Lewis' sudden appearance in the 1954 Cotton Bowl was a strange case of twelve men from one team being on the field at one time. Believe it or not, it happened again, though the circumstances were somewhat different and the time fifteen years later.

It was January 1, 1969, as unbeaten Penn State University went up against the University of Kansas in the Orange Bowl in Miami, Florida. The game was tight from the start and by the fourth period looked as if it would go right down to the wire. With just a little over a minute left and underdog Kansas leading 14–7, the Nittany Lions began a last-ditch drive.

They were moving the ball well and finally exploded for the big play as quarterback Chuck Burkhart found halfback Bob Campbell open and hit him with a pass that covered forty-seven yards before Campbell was stopped on the Kansas three-yard line. With the ball in close, Kansas sent a slew of defensive substitutions onto the field, setting up its goal-line stand.

Penn State took up the challenge, and fullback Tom Cherry cracked into the heart of the Jayhawk line twice. Both times he was stopped for no gain. Then, with just fifteen seconds left, quarterback Burkhart took the snap, saw a hole, and burst through into the end zone for the score. It was 14–13, and Penn State coach Joe Paterno elected to try for a two-point conversion, going for the win rather than a tie.

Again the teams lined up. This time Burkhart dropped back and tried to hit Campbell in the end zone. But the Kansas defense converged and batted the pass away. Jayhawk players hugged each other in jubilation, both on the field and on the sidelines. The game was apparently won.

Or was it? Suddenly the celebration stopped. One of the officials had thrown a penalty flag. He was signaling illegal procedure against Kansas. Now everyone on the Kansas side wanted to know what was wrong, what kind of illegal procedure was being called.

The explanation was simple. The Jayhawks had been playing with twelve men on the field. In fact, they had played the whole sequence from the three with twelve defensive men—the three plays from scrimmage that led to the score, then the play for the extra points. It was an incredible turn of events.

Once the Kansas team regained its composure they realized Penn State would have another chance at the conversion. The teams lined up again, and this time Campbell ran over the left side and into the end zone for two points. Penn State had plucked victory out of nowhere, 15–14!

To this day, no one knows exactly how it happened, how twelve Kansas players had come onto the field and remained there for four plays. At first, the finger pointed to Rick Abernethy, who some thought was supposed to come out on the play. Later Abernethy said, "Nobody told me I was out. There was mass confusion on the field. Penn State was running a hurry-up offense. It was pandemonium out there."

But Abernethy might not have been the twelfth man. Someone was, however, and this amazing foul-up not only embarrassed Kansas, it cost them a victory in the prestigious Orange Bowl. Even more amazing, perhaps, is that no one noticed the violation for three plays. Had it slipped by for one more play, Kansas would have won the game, and it would have taken a sharp-eyed individual watching the films to find the extra man. But it's certainly a prime example of how the unexpected can change the outcome of a ball game.

Then there are times when the bounce of the football takes an odd turn . . . or is it a wrong turn? This one also happened in a Bowl game, the Rose Bowl game played on January 1, 1929, and is the kind of play that would get a barrelful of laughs if it wasn't so crucial to the outcome of a ball game.

The University of California was up against Georgia Tech. In the second period, Tech fumbled the ball at its own 35-yard line, and California defender Roy Riegels scooped it up. Riegels seemed to take a few steps toward the Tech goal, but he bounced off a tackler and somehow lost his bearings. In a split second, Roy Riegels was racing untouched toward his own goal line.

It was a sight to behold, Roy Riegels racing downfield and the only man chasing him . . . one of his teammates. And the big question was, would his teammate catch him in time? Finally, Riegels' teammate Benny Lom caught up with him and stopped him on the 1-yard line. Realizing what he had done, Riegels looked upfield but was immediately buried under a pile of Georgia Tech pursuers.

It was almost a laughable incident, and if it hadn't affected the outcome, it would have been. But with the game still scoreless, Cal decided to punt out of the trouble Riegels had caused. Unfortunately, the kick was blocked and rolled out of the end zone, giving Georgia Tech two points on a safety.

Tech later increased its lead to 8–0 and held on to win, 8–7, the margin of victory the safety which resulted from Roy Riegels's wrong-way run. It was an unexpected happening, and one which Roy Riegels would never forget.

If you think a blunder such as running the wrong way could only happen to an inexperienced college ballplayer, then you're wrong. It can happen to anyone, including an all-pro defensive end. Jim Marshall was among the best at his position in the 1960s and early 1970s, one of the anchors of the famed Minnesota Vikings defensive line, the Purple People Eaters.

But Marshall had his day on the run on October 25, 1964, in a game against the 49ers at San Francisco's Kezar Stadium. It was the fourth period, and the Vikings had a 27–17 lead. San Francisco had the football when quarterback George Mira dumped a short pass off to halfback Billy Kilmer. But Kilmer took just a couple of steps when he fumbled.

The alert Marshall scooped the ball up at the San Francisco 34 and began running. He was the only one in the stadium who didn't realize that he was running the wrong way! Out of his side eye, Marshall noticed the Viking coaches and players all screaming.

"I thought they were cheering me on," he said later.

As he neared the goal line, Marshall recalled thinking that things just didn't seem right. "I remember Fran

Tarkenton (the Vikes quarterback) standing on the sideline and pointing in the opposite direction. I couldn't think of anything else to do, so I threw the ball in the direction of Fran."

What Marshall had done was toss the ball after he had crossed the goal line, and when it rolled out of the end zone before a 49er could recover it, it went as a safety. That made the score 27–19. A San Francisco field goal later made it 27–22, but that's as close as the 'Niners ever got.

Fortunately, Marshall's blunder didn't cost his team the game as Riegels's had done years before. So the fans and players could laugh at it. A few days later, however, Jim Marshall actually received a letter from Roy Riegels, beginning with "Welcome to the club!" Riegels also told Marshall he'd have to learn to laugh at his mistake, because people would be kidding him about it for a long time.

That wasn't the end of it, however. Marshall managed to add some more fuel to the fire. After the season, he was scheduled to fly to Dallas to receive a "Bonehead of the Year" award. What did Jim Marshall do? Simple. He missed the flight and wound up in Chicago!

But it had a happy ending. Not only did Marshall make the ceremony, but he also earned some good off-season bucks speaking and appearing on television, and also through advertisements. And they all came his way because he wasn't sure whether to take a right or a left . . . or a right?

* * *

Talk about making wrong decisions. Here's another one for the books. This one happened on December 23, 1962, as the old Dallas Texans battled the Houston Oilers for the American Football League championship. The AFL was still struggling for respectability in those days. This event didn't help.

It was a hard-fought game from start to finish. In fact, when it was supposed to be over, at the end of the fourth period, the score was tied at 17–17. The game would go into sudden-death overtime, one of the most exciting situations in football. And when it happens in a title game, well, the AFL couldn't have asked for anything more.

In a sudden-death game, there is another coin toss, with the winning team usually choosing to receive, since the first score of any kind wins the game. But Dallas coach Hank Stram decided to take another route. The winds were strong and gusty at Houston's Jeppeson Stadium, and Stram figured it would be to his club's advantage to start the Oilers off with the wind in their face. That way, their great kicker and quarterback, George Blanda, would not be able to use the wind for a long field goal.

Stram instructed his captain, all-league running back Abner Haynes, on just what to say if he won the toss. Sure enough, the coin came up in favor of Dallas. Haynes thought a few seconds as the national television cameras zoomed in.

"We'll kick to the clock," Haynes said.

On the sideline, Coach Stram's face turned a ghostly

white. Haynes had said it wrong. By using the words "we'll kick," he had given up his choice of field position. Not only would Houston receive, but now they chose to have the wind at their backs.

It was a terrible mistake. As Stram said later, Haynes should have simply said they would take this end of the field, facing the clock. He shouldn't have said anything about kicking. Now the Texans were in deep trouble.

Fortunately, the Dallas team had a fine defense, the nucleus of which would move with the team to Kansas City a few years later and, as the K.C. Chiefs, would win Super Bowl IV. And on this day in Houston, the defense did the job. They held the Oilers on several possessions, keeping Blanda out of field-goal range until the first overtime period ended.

Finally, early in the second overtime, with the wind now at their backs, the Texans worked their way downfield and Tommy Brooker booted a 25-yard field goal to win the game and the championship.

But it was Haynes's blunder that got front-page headlines. NFLers, still looking to belittle the new league, had a perfect opportunity. How could a team or a player blow the advantage in a sudden-death overtime? But it happened, unexpected as it was, and for a few years it was remembered more than the eventual Dallas victory.

Though it's almost impossible for anyone to predict the outcome of football games, especially when the two teams are evenly matched, there are certain things that are expected of a team and its star players, especially in the big games. The biggest of the big without a doubt is the Super Bowl. Yet for years, things have somehow turned out other than expected in the big game.

Super Bowl XIX, played on January 20, 1985, was no exception. Everyone agreed that the game was being played between the two best teams in football: the San Francisco 49ers and Miami Dolphins. Everyone also agreed the game would be a matchup between the two top quarterbacks during the 1984 season, veteran Joe Montana of the 49ers and young Dan Marino of the Dolphins.

In fact, the spotlight was really on Marino. He was the new glamour boy of pro football, a second-year quarterback out of the University of Pittsburgh, who had really captured the fancy of the football world.

An all-American at Pitt as a junior, Marino had a sub-par senior season, and for that reason his stock fell with the pro scouts. In a banner year for college quarterbacks, Marino was the seventh chosen, though he was still a first-round draft pick. But by the middle of his rookie year of 1983, he had cracked the Dolphins' starting lineup and played with the polish and poise of a seasoned veteran.

Then came 1984, and Marino practically rewrote the NFL record book. Not only was he the first NFL quarterback to pass for more than 5,000 yards (5,084) in a season, he also obliterated the old record of thirty-six touchdown passes in a season. Marino threw for

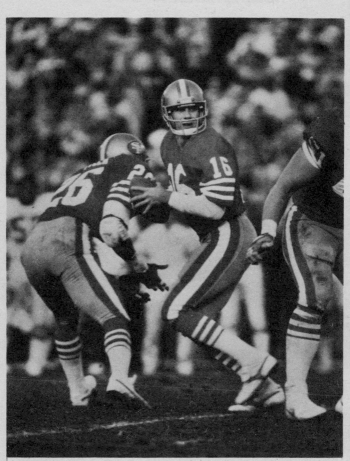

San Francisco's Joe Montana looks downfield in
Super Bowl XIX. Montana was the game's MVP,
leading the 'Niners past the Miami Dolphins and
outplaying the highly publicized young Miami QB,
Dan Marino.

forty-eight. In addition, his 362 completions and four 400-yard passing games were also new league standards. There seemed little he couldn't do when throwing the football, which was early and often. With Marino at the helm, the Dolphins were football's most explosive team.

The 49ers, by contrast, were balanced and deep, with a better defense than the Dolphins and an outstanding quarterback in Montana, who had matured into one of the coolest and most proficient operatives in the league. Everyone expected a real shoot-out, a high-scoring donnybrook that might be won by the team who had the ball last. Many thought the outcome of the game would depend on how well the Dolphin defense contained Montana. No one, they figured, would stop Marino.

It started out according to script. The first time the Dolphins had the ball they began driving. Marino moved them upfield, completing several passes, including a 25-yarder to running back Tony Nathan. The 49er defense stiffened, but Uwe von Schamann hit a 37-yard field goal to put the Dolphins on the board.

The 'Niners then showed Miami it was in for a ball game. Montana led his club on an eight-play, 78-yard drive, utilizing his backs on short passes and running his club over the left side behind 295-pound tackle Bubba Paris. He ended the march with a beautiful 33-yard scoring pass to reserve halfback Carl Monroe. The kick made it a 7–3 game, and it looked to be developing into the shoot-out everyone expected.

When Marino came right back to drive his team in, capping it with a two-yard scoring toss to tight end Dan Johnson, everyone was convinced. The Dolphins led, 10–7, at the end of the quarter, and a real high scorer seemed in the offing.

But at the beginning of the second period things began to change, and once more the specter of the unexpected reared its head. Montana began moving his team better than ever, mixing his own scrambling with runs and passes to his backs and wideouts. An eight-yard scoring pass to fullback Roger Craig ended a 53-yard drive, and a Montana scramble for six yards and a score culminated a 55-yard march. Ray Wersching's conversions made it 21–10, and the crowd of more than 84,000 fans at Stanford Stadium in Palo Alto, California, began buzzing.

When Miami punted for a third straight time, Montana engineered a third straight touchdown drive, Roger Craig carrying over from the two. The kick made it 28–10, as the game was turning into a rout. A pair of von Schamann field goals brought the Dolphins back to 28–16 at the half, but they still weren't looking like the regular-season wrecking crew.

What the 'Niners were doing was shutting down the vaunted Miami passing attack. Their linebackers and secondary were in the process of reducing Dan Marino to a mere mortal. This was totally unexpected. San Francisco linebacker Keena Turner said the team's front four also deserved credit for helping make the defense a total team effort.

"It all started up front," Turner said. "Once our line began pressuring Marino, he couldn't wait as long to throw. Then we could do a better job on the coverage."

Those waiting for a second-half Miami comeback would be sorely disappointed. The 'Niners sacked Marino four times and pressured him countless other times. Yet the young QB kept looking downfield to his wide receivers. The Miami pass catchers were having a tough time with the young, aggressive 'Niner secondary. Plus, Marino was forcing the ball.

So what had been as great a season as a quarterback ever had came unraveled in the finale, the Super Bowl. The San Francisco defense actually shut out the Dolphins over the final two periods while the offense put ten additional points on the board. The final was 38–16, one of the most one-sided Super Bowl games ever played.

The irony of the outcome was that Marino ended up with twenty-nine completions in fifty attempts, both Super Bowl records, and he threw for 318 yards. But he had just one TD and two picked off. Montana, by contrast, completed twenty-four of thirty-five, but for 331 yards and three scores. He also gained 59 yards on five well-timed carries and was named the game's Most Valuable Player.

The outcome also settled, at least for the time being, any questions about the best quarterback in football. Montana played a brilliant game to solidify his position as number one. Marino wasn't so fortunate. Despite his fantastic numbers in '84, he still had a lot to learn. And football fans learned once again that the unexpected can happen at any time and in any game.

Unexpected things have happened in NFL title games for a long time. Go back more than a half century and you'll find one of the most remarkable games ever played. The year was 1934, and it was only the second season that the young National Football League even had a championship game. A year earlier, the Chicago Bears had beaten the New York Giants, 23–21, in a hard-fought contest in Chicago. Now the same two teams were in a rematch, this one in front of some 35,000 fans in New York's Polo Grounds.

It was not a day for football. The weather was frigid, a cold, gusty wind cutting through the stadium. It made the field rock hard, so hard that when the Giants' Ray Flaherty kicked at the ground with his cleats, he didn't even leave a mark. That's when Flaherty made a remark to Giants coach Steve Owen.

"I don't know if this matters, Coach, but we once played on a field like this in college, and we got better traction with basketball shoes instead of cleats."

Owen just nodded but said nothing, and the game began. The Bears were undefeated during the regular season and had beaten the Giants twice. They dominated the first half, but on the frozen field just managed a 10–3 advantage at intermission, the lone touchdown scored on a short plunge by the great Bronko Nagurski.

During half time, Coach Owen remembered the remark about the sneakers. He mentioned it to team trainer Gus Mauch, who quickly put in a call to a friend at Manhattan College. Yes, the friend had a batch of sneakers, and Owen dispatched clubhouse attendant Abe Cohen to get them.

Meanwhile, the game resumed and the Bears continued to dominate, adding a third-period field goal for a 13–3 advantage. But just as the final period began, Abe Cohen returned, carrying an armload of sneakers, with more stuffed into his coat pockets. The Giants players dove into the pile, scrambling for their sizes. Within minutes, the entire Giants team was wearing sneakers.

It was like a magical transformation. With some ten minutes remaining in the game, the Giants stopped their slipping and sliding and began moving more sharply than the Bears, who were still playing in cleats. Within minutes the Giants quarterback Eddie Danowski connected on a 28-yard TD pass with Ike Franklin, closing the gap to 13–10.

The next time the New Yorkers got the football, halfback Ken Strong took over. He roared 42 yards around the end for a score, then kicked the extra point himself to give the Giants a 17–13 lead. It was hard to believe they were the same two teams that had slipped their way through three periods. With their sneakers, the Giants were flying.

And they didn't stop. The next time they got the ball they marched down the field again, mixing runs and passes, their sneakers grabbing the frozen turf as the

Bears tried in vain to stop them. Ken Strong went the final 11 yards on a reverse, making the lead 23–13.

An intercepted pass led to another drive and a 9-yard TD scamper by quarterback Danowski. The kick made it 30–13, and that's the way it ended.

The New York Giants were NFL champions in an incredible turnabout. Who would have dreamed that a change of footwear could have made such a difference? Playing in cleats for the first three periods, the Giants trailed, 13–3, and were being dominated. After changing to sneakers for the final session, the Giants outscored the Bears, 27–0. No doubt at all about the reason. That's why the game has always been referred to as the "Sneakers Game."

Amazing, unexpected things can happen on the football field. This certainly ranks as one of them.

Some players make it and some players don't. Predicting professional careers is a risky business and a place where the unexpected often arises. For instance, there have been a number of top draft choices who have never been able to duplicate their college heroics in the pros. Their careers are nonexistent to mediocre at best.

There have even been a few Heisman Trophy winners who have failed in the pros. The Heisman is given to the man voted the best college player in the land. A couple of notable examples were quarterbacks Gary Beban of UCLA and Terry Baker of Oregon State. Neither played the type of game that was suitable for the NFL. They couldn't pass well enough to cut it as pros, yet they were outstanding in college because their offenses were tailored to their talents.

But even more amazing is the player who comes from nowhere and makes it big. Though it happened more often years ago, when the scouting system wasn't as developed, there was a notable walk-on who wound up in pro football's Hall of Fame.

He walked into the offices of the Los Angeles Rams in the summer of 1952, fresh out of the army, and asked flat out for a job. He had played junior college ball and some service ball, and when the Rams granted him a tryout, Richard Lane made the team.

But it took a while to find his niche. He started on offense but was switched to defense, where he wound up at cornerback. He never quite made it big with the Rams and was finally shipped to the Chicago Cardinals, where his play improved, but he had problems with the coach. Then just before the 1960 season he was traded to the Detroit Lions.

That's where Dick "Night Train" Lane really made his reputation as one of the great cornerbacks in NFL history. Tough, quick, and a gambler, Night Train was a threat to intercept a pass every time out, and he was a deadly tackler as well.

During the course of his fourteen-year career he had sixty-eight lifetime interceptions and a high of fourteen for one year. At one point he was married to the late, great blues singer Dinah Washington, and he had one of the great nicknames in all of sports.

He got the name early in his career, when he was with the Rams. Dick Lane would often visit the room of all-pro receiver Tom Fears to discuss the finer points of the game. Fears was always playing music, and his favorite tune then was "Night Train." Seemed as if every time Lane came to the room, Fears was playing the song. So one night, Fears's roommate, Ben Sheets, saw Lane coming and said, "Here comes Night Train."

Needless to say, it stuck, just as Dick "Night Train" Lane stuck to pass receivers. He was one of the best, and it all started when a skinny kid fresh out of the army walked into the Rams office and asked for a job.

Today, each NFL team has an elaborate scouting system so that even the most obscure ballplayers at every tiny college in the land get a look. Yet, once in a while, the unexpected still happens.

In 1967, the New Orleans Saints used a lowly seventeenth-round pick to take a wide receiver out of Xavier University. As a rule, seventeenth-round draft choices do not survive training camp. But this one did, despite reports that said he was probably too small and too slow. Not only did Dan Abramowicz survive, he became one of the finer receivers of his generation.

Abramowicz was one of those rare receivers who, despite physical limitations, knew how to get open and had a great pair of hands. At one point in his eight-year career he caught passes in 105 straight games, then a record. And during his career with the Saints, 49ers, and Bills, he caught 369 passes for 5,686 yards and thirty-nine touchdowns. Not bad for a seventeenth-round draft choice who wasn't supposed to make it at all.

In 1971, the Baltimore Colts went the Saints one further. They selected a running back as the 441st pick in the entire draft. There were only 442 players chosen that year. Needless to say, no one expected Don Nottingham to make it.

But once in camp, Colt coaches noticed time and again that the defense had trouble stopping the short, squat Nottingham, who soon earned the nickname "the Human Bowling Ball." Sure enough, Nottingham stuck, and while he never became the kind of star Dan Abramowicz did, he made a significant contribution during his seven years in the NFL.

Playing for the Colts and later the Miami Dolphins, Nottingham was a tough, durable player. In 1975, he ground out 718 yards and scored twelve touchdowns for the Dolphins, a fine season for any fullback. He also got to play with Miami in Super Bowl VIII and was part of the Dolphins World Championship team.

Dan Abramowicz and Don Nottingham, two players who were not expected to stick, put in a total of fifteen seasons in the NFL, proving again that the unexpected can happen at any time.

Exciting finishes have long been a special part of football at every level. A game that goes down to the wire can bring fans to the edge of their seats. The winners' jubilation is electric, the losers' dejection dev-

Stanford University's all-America quarterback John Elway shows the classic way to do it in a game during the 1982 season. But when Stanford met California that year, Elway and Company were beaten by one of the wildest kick returns in football history.

astating. Some of these last-minute heroics are the result of good, sound football, a real team effort. But then there are the special few, the finishes that are unexpected, strange, and amazing, all at the same time.

A pair of recent college games not only caught the fancy of the football world but provided the kind of excitement seldom seen at the finish. One involved a number of anonymous players, and the other culminated a duel between a pair of all-American quarterbacks.

The first game took place on November 20, 1982, with Stanford taking on the University of California. It was a hard-fought game from the start, with Stanford the favorite because of the presence of John Elway, one of the top passing quarterbacks in the land.

With California leading, 19–17, and time running out, Elway drove his team downfield. Then with just four seconds left, Stanford kicker Mark Harmon booted a 35-yard field goal to give his team a 20–19 lead. That seemed like a cliff-hanger finish right there. But there was still time for California to receive the kickoff.

Because of an unsportsmanlike-conduct penalty, Stanford had to kick from the 25. Cal's Kevin Moen took the ball at the 43 and started upfield. What followed was one of the strangest, most electrifying, and at the same time confusing plays ever seen.

Moen ran about 10 yards upfield and toward the left sideline as several Stanford players closed in. Suddenly, he lateraled the ball to Richard Rodgers, running behind him. Rodgers crossed midfield and when he saw the enemy close, he lateraled the ball back to Dwight Garner at the Stanford 44. Garner was hit, and as he fell he managed a lateral back to Richard Rodgers at the Stanford 48.

So Rodgers had the ball a second time. He cut back toward midfield and as he was being surrounded, lateraled back to Mariet Ford at the Stanford 46. By now the fans were screaming wildly. They couldn't believe how the football was being passed around like a hot potato. But Ford now had some running room and was sprinting toward the Stanford goal line, where the Cardinal band was already on the field in anticipation of a victory celebration.

Then, at the 25, it looked as if Ford was finally trapped. So what did he do? He threw a blind lateral pass over his right shoulder in a desperation move. Time had run out by now, but the play had to finish before the game could end. The football hung in the air a few seconds, and suddenly Kevin Moen had it again. He was the player who originally fielded the kickoff.

Moen sped toward the end zone as the bewildered Stanford players tried to react. Now the Stanford band came into play. Kevin Moen actually used the members as screens as he neared the goal line. As he crossed the goal line he bowled over a trombone player . . . but no Stanford tacklers could touch him.

For a few seconds confusion reigned. But then the referee signaled a touchdown, and the crowd went wild. There had been five laterals in a 57-yard return, and while there were cries of foul, the TD was allowed to stand, in one of the strangest finishes to a football game ever seen. California thought they had a 19–17 victory; then saw themselves fall behind, 20–19, with four seconds left; and finally made a miracle play to win it, 25–20.

The second noteworthy finish happened on November 23, 1984, as the Eagles of Boston College went up against the Hurricanes of Miami. The game was billed as a shoot-out between two of college football's glamour quarterbacks, B.C.'s Doug Flutie and Miami's Bernie Kosar.

They didn't disappoint. Both signal callers put on a passing show to be remembered for years to come. B.C. led at the quarter, 14–7, and at the half, 28–21. In the third period the two quarterbacks kept throwing, and with one session left, the score was knotted at 31 all. And that still didn't foreshadow the unbelievable finish that was to follow.

First Boston College took a 34–31 lead on a field goal. Then Miami's Melvin Bratton broke loose for a brilliant, 52-yard scoring run that put the Hurricanes out in front, 38–34. Time was now starting to run down. Once again Flutie went to work, driving the Eagles downfield with a mixture of passing and running plays. From the one, Steve Strachan took it in and the kick put B.C. ahead, 41–38.

As time was running out, Kosar took over, and now he drove his team, using the same field generalship that Flutie had shown. The crowd and national television

It was Boston College's Doug Flutie against Miami's Bernie Kosar in a battle of premier signalcallers in December of 1984. Here, Flutie is set to complete one of his passes in that epic battle.

audience couldn't believe it. Could Kosar and Miami pull it out?

Sure enough, Kosar drove the Hurricanes inside the 10, then all the way to the one. With just twenty-eight seconds left, Melvin Bratton went over. Miami had the lead, the kick making it 45–41. It was an amazing finish.

But was it really over? After the kickoff, B.C. had the ball on its own 20 with about twenty seconds left. What miracle could Doug Flutie have left? But the diminutive, 5'9¾" quarterback wasn't about to quit. With the Hurricanes in a prevent defense to stop the long gainer, Flutie passed the Eagles all the way to the Miami 48. The problem was the clock—there was only time for one more play.

Flutie knew he'd have to put it in the end zone. So did Miami, and they had everyone back. At the snap, Flutie dropped back beyond midfield, scrambled to his right to avoid the Hurricane pass rush, then threw the football high and deep and into the end zone.

More than a half dozen Miami and Boston College players went after it. The ball was deflected back into the air . . . and then someone grabbed it. Suddenly, the Boston College players and fans went wild. Flutie's favorite receiver, Gerard Phelan, was clutching the football for a touchdown! The "Hail Mary" pass had worked. Boston College had won the football game with no time left, 47–45, in one of the most miraculous finishes ever.

"All you can do in a case like that is put the ball in

Doug Flutie celebrates one of college football's great endings after his last-second "Hail Mary" pass was caught in the end zone to give his club the victory.

the end zone," Flutie said. "We've got our guys down there, and they've got their guys back there. You just have to see who comes up with it."

As for the quarterback shoot-out, it was everything and more. Flutie had completed thirty-four of forty-six passes for 472 yards and three scores. Kosar wasn't far behind with twenty-five completions in thirty-eight attempts for 447 yards and two scores. The game featured two of college football's best quarterbacks at the top of their game, as well as one of the most exciting, unexpected finishes in the game's history. Who could ask for anything more?

All Around the Gridiron

Funny, strange, and amazing things are constantly happening on the football field at every level of competition. Many of these events can't really be put in a category. They just stand on their own for what they are.

Taking a trip all around the gridiron reveals just how different the sport of football has been at any given time down through the years. As always, these incredible happenings can involve the great, the near great, or the obscure players who are long forgotten.

Tony Dorsett is one of the most consistently explosive running backs ever to play the game. In 1985, at the age of thirty-one, Dorsett was still churning out the yards for the Dallas Cowboys, the hub of their running attack as he has been since his rookie year of 1977. But

Dorsett was a star long before he began playing for the pros. In fact, he had an amazing streak that really proved his excellence as a runner. But even stranger than that was the way his streak was finally stopped.

The streak involves the ultimate barometer for all running backs—the 1,000-yard season. Beginning with his junior year at Hopewell High School in Aliquippa, Pennsylvania, Tony Dorsett began stringing together 1,000-yard campaigns. He did it as a junior and senior at Hopewell, then went to the University of Pittsburgh.

Though freshmen were eligible for varsity ball by the time Dorsett became a Panther in 1973, not that many cracked the starting lineup. Dorsett not only cracked it, he became an all-American. As a 155-pound running back, Tony gained 1,586 yards on 288 carries. He was on his way to becoming the first college player to run for more than 1,000 yards four straight years, culminating it with 1,948 yards his senior year, when his team won the National Championship and he captured the coveted Heisman Trophy.

Drafted by the Cowboys, Dorsett was not a starter until midway through his rookie season; yet he wound up with 1,007 yards to keep the streak going. It was his seventh straight 1,000-yard season beginning in high school. It was also the start of his five straight 1,000-yard seasons for the Cowboys.

So coming into 1982, Tony Dorsett had an incredible

Mr. 1,000-yard runner. Tony Dorsett of the Cowboys running to daylight against the Steelers in Super Bowl XIII. Except for the players' strike in 1982, Dorsett has gained 1,000 yards every season since his high school days.

string of eleven consecutive years in which he gained the magic number of yards. He was coming off a 1981 campaign which was his best as a pro. He ran for some 1,646 yards. Then, in 1982, the streak ended!

How did it end? Did the defenses catch up with Tony Dorsett? Was his age beginning to show? Did an injury finally put him on the shelf? Sorry, it was none of the above. What finally stopped Tony Dorsett from gaining his customary 1,000 yards was . . . a players' strike!

Yes. The 1982 season was shortened to nine games by the strike, and Tony managed to gain just 745 yards. It was still good enough to lead the NFC, and without the strike, he certainly would have made it. The next year he quickly returned to the 1,000-yard fold, and did it again in 1984 and 1985.

So if it hadn't been for that strike, Tony would have completed his fifteenth consecutive 1,000-yard season in 1985. Strike or no, Tony Dorsett is one of the best, and this running back has the stats to prove it.

While 1,000 yards has always been the norm for a Tony Dorsett, the magical mark has proved to be quite elusive for other runners. But perhaps no one had the kind of incredible frustration in trying to get there than Dave Hampton, who played with the Atlanta Falcons in the mid-1970s.

Hampton was a solid, if not spectacular, back who began his NFL career with Green Bay. Never quite able to crack the starting lineup with the Pack,

Hampton gained just 787 yards in his first three years. But after he was traded to the Falcons, he came into his own.

In the final game of 1972, Hampton was on the brink of every runner's goal—the 1,000-yard season. He was running well that day, and the statisticians kept careful track of his running. In the fourth period after another Hampton carry, the game was stopped. Dave Hampton had his 1,000 yards, and he was given the game ball. But on his next carry, Hampton was thrown for a six-yard loss. Suddenly, he was below 1,000 again. With time running down, he got the ball just one more time, but was stopped after a gain of one.

Game ball in hand, Hampton was given the bad news. He had just 995 yards because of that six-yard loss. He hadn't made it after all, a disappointing and embarrassing situation for the fourth-year pro. He was determined to do it the next season, 1973.

Once again it came down to the final game. Hampton had 913 yards going in and needed 87 to reach 1,000. The Falcons kept calling his number, again and again. He was to carry the football twenty-seven times that day . . . but wouldn't you know it, he gained just 84 yards. Once again Dave Hampton fell short, this time with 997 yards for the season!

Ironically, the scenario was the same in 1975. Hampton had 941 yards going into the final game. This time he finally made it, but only by the skin of his teeth. This time he managed to rush for 61 yards to finish with 1,002 yards for the year. It was a three-year struggle, but Dave Hampton had finally done it. It must have been quite a relief.

Take a talented athlete, give him a nickname that somehow catches the fancy of the public, and there's no limit to the amazing things that can happen to him. Especially if he's a member of a football team that loses just one game all year and winds up winning the Super Bowl!

The athlete is William Perry. The team is the Chicago Bears. And the nickname is "The Refrigerator."

There probably isn't a football fan anywhere who doesn't know the Refrigerator by now. He's 6' 2", 308-pound defensive tackle who was the Bears' first-round draft choice prior to the 1985 season. The Fridge was a two-time all-American nose guard at Clemson University, and was expected to become an instant star in the NFL. But, when he reported to training camp, there were those who thought William Perry had opened the refrigerator door a few times too often.

One of twelve children, this native of Aiken, S.C. weighed 13 pounds at birth—not a bad beginning—and by the time he entered the seventh grade he was up to a devastating 220. A year later, he was pushing 240 and when he joined the Clemson Tigers in the fall of 1981, he was over the 300-pound mark. His nickname, the Refrigerator, was a natural.

There were times during his college days when the Refrigerator's weight was pushing the 370 mark. Yet this amazing all-around athlete was still agile enough to dunk a basketball. And, by the time he finished wreaking havoc in the Atlantic Coast Conference, all the pros wanted him. But it was the Bears who got him.

When he walked into the Chicago training camp in the summer of 1985, some thought he looked more like a frozen-food locker than a simple refrigerator. And the Bears' defensive coordinator, Buddy Ryan, quickly dismissed him by saying the team had wasted a number-one draft choice. That was a low point, maybe the only low point, William Perry was to know all year. The rest of his season was simply incredible.

First came the hard work, the work that got William back to being a simple refrigerator, at about 308 pounds. Next came the job of learning his trade, as a defensive tackle in the NFL. By mid-season he had earned a starting job on a team headed for the Super Bowl.

The Bears were full of stars and personalities, such as running back Walter Payton, quarterback Jim McMahon, linebacker Mike Singletary, and defensive end Richard Dent. But before long, the Refrigerator was as well known as any of them.

His star rose even further when coach Mike Ditka began using him as a fullback in goal-line situations. He was either a battering-ram blocker for Payton or a bull of a ball carrier. When William scored a touchdown in a victory over Green Bay, he made national headlines and all of the highlight films. Then, in later games, he went on to score a couple of more times, once by catching a pass. Now, the legend of Refrigerator Perry had really been born.

The Bears finished the regular season with a 15–1 record, and in the playoffs, fans of the opposing teams were after the Refrigerator. Before the Bears met the New York Giants, some of the Giants' rooters lined up a number of old refrigerators and crushed them with a Bigfoot truck. They said that was the way their team was going to crush Refrigerator Perry.

But no one did. In the Super Bowl, he was a force, blocking and tackling like a demon, and delighting the Bears' fans by scoring a touchdown on a short run. When he was under a full head of steam, no one man could hope to stop him.

It was truly an amazing season for William Perry. At the outset, he was pressured to lose weight. He did it. Then he had to learn the Bears' system and a new position. He did it. After that, they asked him to play some offense. He did it. When his nickname caught on, he was asked to appear both in commercials and on live television. He did it.

And through it all, he improved as a football player, and became an important part of a Super Bowl–winning team. You can't have a rookie year much more amazing than that.

One of the most cherished of all children's stories is *Heidi*, a warm and inspiring tale of a small girl and her grandfather in the Swiss Alps. But did you know there was a time when *Heidi* defeated both the Oakland Raiders and New York Jets, and caused a nationwide scandal?

It happened on November 17, 1968. That was the day the Raiders and Jets engaged in an epic battle at the Oakland-Alameda County Coliseum. The Jets, en route to their first American Football League division title, were led by their flamboyant young quarterback, Joe Namath. The Raiders presented their usual cast of tough football players, many of whom didn't like all the publicity Namath was getting. The game was a brutal battle from the opening kickoff.

Besides that, it was a close football game, with the outcome in doubt all the way. It was 14–12 Oakland at the half, and 22–19 in favor of the Raiders at the end of three. But then Broadway Joe went to work, hitting his favorite receiver, Don Maynard, on a nifty 50-yard touchdown pass, giving the Jets the lead at 26–22. The Raiders, however, came right back on a 22-yard TD toss from Daryle Lamonica to Fred Biletnikoff. Now Oakland was back on top, 29–26. It was that kind of game.

Then a pair of Jim Turner field goals put the Jets in front again, 32–29, the last coming with just over one minute left in the game. The clock on the wall hit seven just as Turner made the go-ahead field goal, when suddenly, on all the TV sets east of Denver, the game went off and the credits for the start of *Heidi* appeared.

Shocked football fans didn't know what to think. All the Jets had to do was hold the Raiders for a minute

Broadway Joe Namath fires downfield as his Jets confront the Oakland Raiders in 1968. With the Jets ahead late in the game, NBC cut to a production of *Heidi,* and enraged football fans didn't get to see a miraculous Raider comeback in the final seconds.

and they would win. They probably did that, most fans thought. But still . . . *Heidi!* It didn't seem fair.

Then the real kicker hit. As fans turned on their radios to hear the final score confirmed, they couldn't believe what had happened. Just seconds after the game went off and Heidi began to frolic on screen, Daryle Lamonica had thrown a 43-yard touchdown pass to Charlie Smith. Suddenly, the Raiders had a 36–32 lead in a game most viewers thought the Jets had won.

And that wasn't all. On the ensuing kickoff, the Jets' Earl Christy fumbled the ball on his own 2-yard line. Oakland's Preston Ridlehuber scooped the ball up and ran it into the end zone for still another Raider touchdown. The kick made it 43–32, and *that's* the way the game ended.

Once fans learned about the Raiders' two-touchdown lightning strike, the network's switchboards became jammed by irate fans. Never before had the gridiron game caused such a stir with a major television network. In New York, fans also called the newspapers, other TV stations, and the police. Many of the callers still weren't sure how the game had ended, and when they found out they became even more enraged.

Finally, the network president was forced to issue a public apology. He said that he, too, was disappointed by not seeing the end of the game. He also said that the network wanted to keep the game on, but that their communication system had broken down, and by the time the message got through, the game had truly ended.

Though the Jets went on to win the AFL title and then Super Bowl III in a titanic upset, many fans never forgot the infamous *Heidi* game. And they never let the network forget. After that, the late-afternoon football games always aired to their conclusion, no matter how one-sided, with regular programming pushed back to accommodate the heroes of the gridiron. And that's really the way it should be. Right, football fans?

The *Heidi* game might have proved that even television networks cannot turn a deaf ear to the desires of the fans, but there once was a player whose deaf ear almost cost him a career. He was running back Larry Brown, drafted out of Kansas State by the Washington Redskins in 1969.

Brown had been more of a blocker than a runner in college, so he didn't have big stats as an advertisement. But the Skins knew he was a hard worker and they picked him on the eighth round, a position that doesn't ordinarily produce big stars.

But it was Larry Brown's work ethic that got him through his first training camp and most impressed Coach Vince Lombardi, who had taken over the Redskins that year. There was one problem, however. Larry just didn't get off fast. A good back has to react quickly at the snap and get into that hole. Larry Brown would always hesitate a split second before coming off the ball, and it was affecting his running.

For a time, Lombardi and his staff thought that perhaps Larry just didn't have it to be a top runner. But then they discovered the problem. Larry Brown was almost totally deaf in one ear. Therefore, whenever he lined up with that ear closer to the quarterback, he couldn't hear the signals, and that was causing the hesitation.

Coach Lombardi had to see NFL Commissioner Pete Rozelle for permission to install a special hearing aid inside Larry's helmet. That done, Larry Brown became a full-fledged star, a 1,000-yard runner who always gave his all to help his team.

He was the only player in the NFL to wear a special $400 helmet during practice and in games. But for the results it achieved, the helmet was a very cheap investment, indeed.

Every football fan knows about Terry Bradshaw, the former quarterback of the Pittsburgh Steelers. During the course of his NFL career, blond-haired Bradshaw led his team to an unprecedented four Super Bowl championships. He was a great leader with a great throwing arm.

But Bradshaw's throwing arm was not discovered on the gridiron. While he was already playing football in high school, his arm drew raves for an accomplishment in another sport. In the spring of 1966, Terry was a member of the Shreveport (Louisiana) Woodlawn High School track team. There weren't many people around as he got ready for his specialty—throwing the javelin.

Pittsburgh quarterback Terry Bradshaw ready to rifle a pass downfield during Super Bowl XIII. Bradshaw led his club to four Super Bowl triumphs in the 1970's, but few people know that one of his longest throws was made with a javelin.

The big youngster came down the runway with a perfect approach and let fly. The javelin left his hand like a blue blur and sailed upward. At the point where the other competitors' throws would start coming down, Bradshaw's toss was still rising. Those watching gasped in awe, and meet officials had the feeling something very extraordinary was happening.

When the spear finally buried its tip in the ground, officials rushed out with the tape. They couldn't believe their eyes. Terry Bradshaw had thrown the javelin 243 feet, 7 inches. He had set a new national prep school record by some 11 feet!

So it was no surprise when Terry Bradshaw later showed the pros he could throw a football through a brick wall. He always had a great arm, and he proved it early in a very amazing way.

Today, football teams at every level dream of a quarterback with an arm like a Terry Bradshaw. But there was a time when it didn't matter, because the forward pass wasn't really part of the game. As amazing as that sounds, it's true.

Just when was the first forward pass used in a football game? It's hard to say. One story goes back to the Yale-Princeton game of 1876. Others point to various college games played before the turn of the century. But any kind of pass thrown in these games was more or less a freak play, almost an accident. No one bothered to develop a real passing attack until the early part of the twentieth century.

Strangely enough, one of the men involved is well remembered, all right, but not as a player. He was Knute Rockne, who became perhaps the most legendary college coach ever when he led his great Notre Dame teams of the 1920s and 1930s. As a coach, Rockne was a great innovator, as well as a great motivator. But as a player, he was an innovator, too.

The Rock was an end on the 1912 and 1913 Notre Dame teams, and somewhere at the start of that period, he and his quarterback, Charles "Gus" Dorais, began talking about the value of the forward pass as an offensive weapon. Soon the two were practicing together, Rockne running the pass patterns and Dorais hitting him on the break, just as the modern-day passers do it.

When the Fighting Irish traveled to West Point for a game with powerful Army in 1913, Rockne and Dorais decided to put their newly devised passing game to the test. The Cadets expected the old-fashioned running game, with tight line play and bruising blocks up front. So when the two Notre Damers opened it up, it took Army completely by surprise.

Dorais completed thirteen of seventeen passes for 243 yards, with Rockne on the receiving end of most of them. The Irish won easily, 35–13, with all five of their touchdowns either set up or scored by Dorais's passing. It was truly an amazing game for its day.

Despite Notre Dame's big passing day, it still took many more years before either the colleges or pros would accept the passing game on a large scale. But two innovative and daring players had laid the groundwork early with deadly accuracy.

Crazy pranks and practical jokes have long been a part of the sports scene, and football has had its share. One of the great jokers in pro football was Wayne Walker, who played outside linebacker for the Detroit Lions in the 1960s. Walker was an unlikely source to create premeditated mayhem. He was perhaps the finest outside linebacker of his time, an intelligent ballplayer, a student of the game, and a leader on the field.

But Walker picked his moments to have fun. He and the Lions all-pro middle linebacker, Joe Schmidt, once donned vampire costumes that Schmidt and his wife had worn to a masquerade party. They paraded around training camp at three in the morning and scared half their teammates out of their wits.

Another time he sent an unsuspecting rookie down to a local supermarket, telling him that all members of the Lions were entitled to a free turkey. The strange part was that when the rookie went in and demanded his turkey, the store owner actually gave him one.

But there was a time when Walker was a rookie that he ended up on the receiving end of the laughs. The team was working out at Hollywood High. They would leave their hotel in shorts and T-shirts and walk to the practice field, where a couple of hundred people would be waiting to watch. One day the gate was locked, so

Walker, being a rookie, was told to climb a spiked fence so he could get someone inside to open the gate.

"I got up on the fence," Walker said, "but my shorts got caught on a spike and it took them right off. There were 200 people there, and my teammates were all cheering. I don't think I ever ran faster in my life in getting to the caretaker's house."

So there are plenty of funny days, even for the rough, tough men who play in the NFL.

There's an old baseball expression that goes "good field, no hit." It describes a player who contributes very little with the bat, but makes up for it with his outstanding glove. To take some liberties and transpose the expression to the gridiron, it might go something like "good defense, no offense."

If that were a tried-and-true football expression, it would perfectly describe the 1938 Duke University football team. For that Blue Devil squad produced one of the strangest seasons on record. And it all came down to a matter of good defense, no offense.

In fact, the Blue Devils had a great defense that year, a super defense, so outstanding that no one could score a single point against them in the regular season. It was the defense that kept the team in every single ball game and enabled the anemic offense to do just enough to win.

The Duke gridders ended the regular season with a perfect 9–0 record. Yet in five of the nine games, the offense scored seven or fewer points, and that's generally not enough offense to earn a .500 record. But because the defense was absolutely perfect, the team was perfect, too.

So the Blue Devils ended up traveling to Pasadena, California, where on January 2, 1939, they went up against the Trojans of Southern California in the prestigious Rose Bowl. And for most of the game, the same pattern prevailed. The Duke offense did next to nothing, but the defense yielded absolutely nothing!

For three periods the game was scoreless. Then, early in the final session, Duke's Tony Ruffa booted a 23-yard field goal to give the Blue Devils a 3–0 lead. With their unyielding defense, that looked as if it would be enough. Then, with time running down, USC moved the ball to the Duke 34.

That's when the USC coaching staff made a surprising move. At the suggestion of an assistant coach, a fourth-string quarterback named Doyle Nave was sent into the game, along with a substitute receiver named Al Krueger. After a penalty moved the ball back to the 39, Nave and Krueger showed what they were in the game for. Nave threw three straight passes to Krueger, the first gaining thirteen yards to the 26, the second nine, to the 17, while the third lost two yards to the 19.

Then, with just forty-one seconds remaining in the game, Nave looked to pass again. He spotted Krueger heading for the end zone and fired. Touchdown! Al Krueger had grabbed Nave's pass in the Duke end zone. They had done what no team had been able to do all season—score on the Blue Devil defense.

It was a shocking turn. The Duke defense had held its opponents scoreless for 599 minutes and 19 seconds of a 600-minute season. But those last 41 seconds cost dearly. USC won the game, 7–3; ended Duke's hopes of an unbeaten year and a Rose Bowl triumph; and most of all put the only blemish on one of the most amazing defensive accomplishments ever. Now if only they had an offense . . .

Whether you like it or whether you don't, the weather has often played a major role in National Football League championship games. With the advent of the Super Bowl and the modern era, some of the guessing has been eliminated. The Super Bowl, for instance, has always been played at a neutral, warm-weather site, so there will be no midwinter disaster in Minnesota, Green Bay, Chicago, or even New York.

In addition, many cold-weather cities are constructing domed stadiums. The Silverdome, in Pontiac, Michigan, and the home of the Detroit Lions, has already hosted a Super Bowl because there was no chance of the severe Michigan weather creeping inside.

But the 1940s were a different story. It seemed that the weather was a factor in almost every NFL championship. Sure, it happened earlier as well, such as in the famous sneakers game of 1934. But by the 1940s, passing was a big part of the game, and when the weather was foul, the game lost a lot more than it had previously.

In 1945, the Washington Redskins traveled to Cleveland for the NFL title game against the old Cleveland Rams. The week before the game, a monster cold wave roared into the midwest. Rams' owner Dan Reeves tried to keep the playing field from freezing by covering it with nine thousand bales of hay. Then he had a tarpaulin put over the hay.

That was fine, until a blizzard descended and tons of snow covered the tarp and the hay. Reeves then had to hire some three hundred men to try to clear the field in time. When they did, it was discovered that the ground had frozen anyway. Plus a killer wind came whipping off Lake Erie the day of the game, and it ended up costing both Washington and Cleveland.

What it cost the Redskins was the ball game. A gust of wind caught one of Sammy Baugh's passes and blew it into the goalposts. Because of an obscure NFL rule, the pass became a safety. It gave the Rams two points, just enough for their 15–14 victory.

What it cost Cleveland was its franchise. Fed up with the bad weather and the way it affected attendance, owner Reeves moved his club to Los Angeles. Of course, the city of Cleveland only mourned briefly. Several years later they got another franchise, the Browns, and their success story is well known. The Rams also prospered in their new home. So the move was good for everyone, whether they liked it or not.

Then there was the 1948 game between the Philadelphia Eagles and Chicago Cardinals. This one was played at old Shibe Park in Philadelphia. The problem: snow. It snowed and snowed and snowed. The field was covered, the stands were covered, most of the 36,309 fans were covered. The game was little more than slipping and sliding.

The only score came early in the fourth quarter when the Eagles recovered a Chicago fumble on the Cardinal 17. Several plays later Steve Van Buren blasted over for a TD and the kick made it a 7–0 game, which was the way it ended. None of the Eagles players ever wanted to see that kind of snow again.

Imagine how relieved the Eagles must have been the following year when they again won the Eastern Division and learned they would be playing the title game against the Rams in sunny, dry California. Couldn't ask for more, right?

Wrong. There was a rare rainstorm in L.A. the day of the game. And what a storm. It never stopped, and the Eagles found themselves going from the Snow Bowl one year to the Drench Bowl the next. The field was a muddy quagmire, footing next to impossible. But Eagles quarterback Tommy Thompson managed a 31-yard TD pass to Pete Pihos in the second period, and defensive end Leo Skladany blocked a Ram punt and took it into the end zone in the third period.

The rest of the game belonged to the great Eagles running back, Steve Van Buren. While everyone else slipped and slid and slogged through the mud, Van Buren ran. The weather didn't seem to affect him, and he controlled the ball and the game. Philly won, 14–0, and Steve Van Buren set an incredible record by gaining 196 yards on thirty-one carries, piling up more offense than the entire Rams team.

So while football has changed in many ways over the years, don't forget about the weather. It's still a factor every now and then, but with artificial surfaces, domed stadiums, and neutral sites, it's not the way it used to be, when players would wake up the day of a title game never knowing what to expect. The result was often funny, strange, and sometimes amazing . . . just like so many other things in the world of the gridiron.

About the Author

BILL GUTMAN has been an avid sports fan ever since he can remember. A freelance writer for fourteen years, he has done profiles and bios of many of today's sports heroes. Although Mr. Gutman likes all sports, he has written mostly about baseball and football. Currently, he lives in Poughquag, New York, with his wife, two step-children, seven dogs, and five birds.